SELECTED POEMS

SIR THOMAS WYATT was born in Kent in 1503 and spent most of his life in the service of King Henry VIII. In 1520 he married Elizabeth Brooke and the following year their son was born. The marriage was not a success and five or six years later Wyatt separated from his wife. It is possible that at this time he became involved in a relationship with Anne Boleyn. Wyatt first showed his diplomatic skills on a mission to France in 1526; in 1537 he was appointed ambassador to the court of the emperor Charles V. In 1541, however, Wyatt was imprisoned in the Tower of London on a charge of treason. Although the allegations were never substantiated, Wyatt had to confess to his guilt and return to his wife as a condition of his release. In 1542 he was sent by the king to escort a Spanish envoy from Falmouth to London. He died of a fever brought on by the journey.

HARDIMAN SCOTT was born in 1920. After working as a newspaper journalist, he joined the BBC where he became a distinguished political correspondent and editor. He was also the author of a number of books of poetry, and four detective novels. Hardiman Scott was president of the Suffolk Poetry Society from 1979 to 1999. He died in 1999.

Fyfield*Books* aim to make available some of the great classics of British and European literature in clear, affordable formats, and to restore often neglected writers to their place in literary tradition.

Fyfield*Books* take their name from the Fyfield elm in Matthew Arnold's 'Scholar Gypsy' and 'Thyrsis'. The tree stood not far from the village where the series was originally devised in 1971.

> *Roam on! The light we sought is shining still.*
> *Dost thou ask proof? Our tree yet crowns the hill,*
> *Our Scholar travels yet the loved hill-side*

from 'Thyrsis'

SIR THOMAS WYATT

Selected Poems

Edited with an introduction by
HARDIMAN SCOTT

Fyfield*Books*

CARCANET

First published in Great Britain in 1996 by
Carcanet Press Limited
Alliance House
Cross Street
Manchester M2 7AQ

This impression 2003

A CIP catalogue record for this book is available from the British Library
ISBN 1 85754 695 4

The publisher acknowledges financial assistance from
the Arts Council of England

Printed and bound in England by SRP Ltd, Exeter

Contents

To my friends of the
Suffolk Poetry Society

Introduction

Sir Thomas Wyatt stands at a crossroads in English poetry. He inherits the best of a medieval lyric tradition and, at the same time, points forward to the achievement of the Elizabethans. For the reader of today he is a modern poet before his time.

He introduced to England *terza rima*, *ottava rima*, and the sonnet, almost creating the form which has become known as the Shakespearean sonnet. Only in this century, however, has he been regarded as at least equal, if not superior, to his younger contemporary, Henry Howard, Earl of Surrey. In English literature Surrey may be of greater historic importance, since his introduction of blank verse provided the measure for Shakespeare's plays and has had a lasting influence on English poetry. The originality of Wyatt, however, suggests to the modern reader that he was not only a surprising innovator in poetry but, in Professor Kenneth Muir's words, 'the first great English lyric poet'.

Thomas Wyatt was born at Allington Castle, Kent, in 1503. He died 39 years later. He was the son of Sir Henry Wyatt, whose loyalty to Henry Tudor led to his imprisonment and torture under Richard III. When Henry VII came to the throne he rewarded such loyalty, and Sir Henry served both him and Henry VIII in a number of appointments. His son, Thomas, was also to spend his life either at Court or in the service of the Court. He inherited his father's steadfast loyalty, writing in one poem [14]: 'My king, my country, alone for whom I live...' His first office at Court was in 1516. He went to Cambridge, probably to St John's College, where he took an MA, and thence again to Court. He was considered handsome by his contemporaries, and soon proved himself a daring knight who enjoyed the king's favour. He became a distinguished soldier and scholar, a linguist and skilled diplomat, a poet whose works were admired at Court, and most likely a lutenist as well.

In 1520, he married Elizabeth Brooke, the daughter of Lord Cobham, and the following year his son, also Thomas, was born.

It was not a happy marriage and five or six years later he separated from her because of her adultery. About this time he was attracted to Anne Boleyn, and they may have been lovers, although one of Anne's maids, Anne Gainsford, says that her mistress 'rejected all his speech of love'. Whatever the truth of the matter, it seems certain that some kind of relationship existed, and equally certain that it ended as soon as Wyatt discovered that the king wanted her. (The first poem, a sonnet, in this selection refers to this.)

Soon Wyatt was deep into his diplomatic career. Early in 1526 he went to France with Sir Thomas Cheyney to negotiate the part England would play in the Holy League of Cognac. It was something short of full membership because of French threats to British trade. In any event the League did nothing to prevent the victories of the Emperor Charles V in Italy. Wyatt, in spite of Henry VIII's impossible policies, showed his diplomatic skills in missions to that country, and managed to escape when he was captured by Spanish troops.

Some ten years later (1537) the king made Wyatt ambassador to the court of the Emperor, Charles V. The object was to prevent an alliance between France and Spain, to improve the Emperor's relations with Henry, and to discover the likelihood of an attack upon England. The Pope had by now excommunicated Henry and had appointed Cardinal Reginald Pole to organize an attack upon England by continental countries. Wyatt followed Charles, with whom he had established a better relationship than most, wherever he went through France and Spain. Two clerics, Bonner and Haynes, were sent to help Wyatt, but were a great deal more nuisance than they were worth. In despatches to London, Bonner made charges against Wyatt's behaviour. Thomas Cromwell, Wyatt's patron and friend, ignored them. After Cromwell's fall from power, however, these allegations were to resurface in 1541, and Wyatt was imprisoned in the Tower on a charge of treason.

There was not the slightest substance in the charges, and Wyatt defended himself with eloquent vigour and wit in a letter to the

Privy Council and in a speech to his trial judges. There is, however, no record of the trial having taken place. Even so, and in spite of Wyatt's innocence, it is unlikely that he would have survived but for Queen Katherine Howard's plea to the King. The double sonnet [9] and an epigram [15] describe Wyatt's physical and mental state during his imprisonment. The conditions for his release were unpleasant. Wyatt had to confess his guilt and return to his wife. Adulterous relations would result in his death and the confiscation of his property. For the past five years he had been living happily with Elizabeth Darrell, the daughter of Sir Edward Darrell. Within the year Queen Katherine herself was executed for adultery.

Wyatt had been in prison on two previous occasions: briefly in 1534 for an affray with the Sergeants of London, during which one was killed; and for six weeks in 1536, at the same time as Anne Boleyn and her lovers were in the Tower. The reason for his arrest is not clear, but evidently the Duke of Suffolk had something to do with it. From his cell Wyatt probably saw Anne's execution.

Wyatt's last diplomatic mission ended in his death. In October 1542 a Spanish envoy arrived at Falmouth sooner than expected. Because of his experience and the Spaniards' trust in him, Wyatt was sent by the King to escort the envoy to London. Wyatt rode as hard as he could with relays of horses. He became overheated, developed a fever, and died, most likely of pneumonia, in the home of his friend, Sir Thomas Horsey, at Sherborne. He was buried there, and a plaque marks his tomb.

Wyatt's diplomatic missions abroad familiarized him with the work of French and Italian poets. Scholars have traced the influence of Petrarch, Serafino, Alamanni and Trissino, but it was an influence which he completely absorbed. Of equal if not more importance was the example of Chaucer.

Wyatt took from Petrarch the sonnet and brought it to England, but few of the sonnets are literal translations. For the most part they are adaptations and imitations, and others are wholly original works. Frequently, Petrarch is no more than a starting point

11

for Wyatt. His attitude to women and his treatment of them in verse is quite different from Petrarch's. Wyatt's poems of courtly love are unconventional. The lady's beauty is not even mentioned, and faithlessness, wiliness and cruelty by the lady are not accepted with loving devotion. Wyatt, indeed, expresses his unhappiness and his pain, but he is quite outspoken in his reactions and in his sense of injustice. If he considers the lady blameworthy, he blames her, and sometimes she is made to suffer for her own cruelty [12]. In 'Blame not my lute' [19] he tells his lady, in the fifth stanza, to blame herself, and until she changes her behaviour, his lute will play the truth about her. And in his most anthologized poem, 'My lute, awake!' [18] he promises the lady that her rejection of his love, and her unkindness to other lovers, will exact vengeance in the future and cause her to repent the time she 'hast lost and spent'. Samuel Daniel copied the theme closely in his sonnet, 'When men shall find thy flow'r'.

A number of Wyatt's lyrics were doubtless written within the convention of courtly love, and some might have been prompted by his relations with young women at Court. They would have been sung, perhaps to popular tunes or improvised melodies, or passed round in collections of poems to be read. But it would be a mistake to over-emphasize this social activity. The context in which his poems were written embraced not only Henry VIII's revival of entertainment, revelry and music, but also the insecurity of life at his Court and the dangers inherent in any service to the King. This is evidenced in such a poem as 'Take heed betime lest ye be spied' [56]. Wyatt used the convention of courtly love for the expression of attitudes and values that were not characteristic of that convention. For example, his devotion to truth and to loyalty, his need for true love, fidelity, kindness, security, and his belief in the necessity for honesty.

This is apparent in one of Wyatt's best known but more difficult poems, 'They flee from me' [28]. It has attracted extensive studies, especially in America, offering a variety of interpretations. Wyatt's very conciseness does sometimes, as in this poem, lead to ambiguity or obscurity. But there is no denying that he

12

is occupied with the nature of human behaviour, its possibilities, its frailties and its fickleness. Although the poem shares the same rhyme scheme as *Troilus and Criseyde*, it is rhythmically subtler than Chaucer's decasyllables.

In the sonnet, 'I abide and abide' [10] Wyatt advises his lady that it is better to speak the truth plainly than to tell him to abide and then to refuse him. His adherence to faithfulness and to truth lies behind many of the poems and is specifically expressed in 'Perdie, I said it not' [24]; and 'If thou wilt mighty be' [29] epitomizes the values he holds dear. In effect, the poem says that if man is guided by sensual desire he cannot govern himself; God has made him noble, but if he is conquered by lust and vice and a covetous concern for wealth, then nothing can prevent life being wretched. But only he is wretched who thinks himself so, and Wyatt will not succumb to it: 'No, no, I live and must do still,' he writes in another poem [50], which also has this characteristic assertion: 'Who hath himself shall stand upright'.

So Wyatt is frequently using the convention of courtly love not to play the courtly game with its expression of conventional emotions, but to define and express his own personal emotions. In this he is quite original. It is the nearest thing in sixteenth-century poetry to what, in modern times, has become known as confessional verse.

The other distinctly modern attribute of Wyatt's poetry is its conversational style. He uses the words of everyday speech in conversational cadences. This led early critics to describe his prosody as rough. They assumed he was struggling to achieve metrical regularity. Even C.S. Lewis (in Volume III of the *Oxford History of English Literature*) says Wyatt's metres are 'what we should expect in a man who was escaping from the late medieval swamp; first his floundering and then, after conversion, his painful regularity'. Lewis does concede, however, that Wyatt's lyrics escape these strictures. Today it is easier to see Wyatt as a consummate craftsman who, like any poet, would occasionally have his off-day.

The expression of his own emotions, personal reactions and

13

opinions could not be most powerfully conveyed in the regular metrical compositions which were then becoming popular and which are to be found in their most accomplished form in the poems of Henry Howard. Wyatt was not striving to achieve metrical regularity and to write in smooth iambic pentameters. But he shows so much skill in handling words in a variety of rhythms that if he had wanted to write regular pentameters he clearly could have done so.

Coleridge, in the *Biographia Literaria*, reminded us 'that poetry of the highest kind may exist without metre'. The structure of Wyatt's poetry is much closer to what has been called 'organic form'. Any difficulty in reading him disappears if one forgets metre, and pauses where the natural rhythms of speech indicate a pause. The rhythm then is determined by conversational phrases. Moreover, Raymond Southall has convincingly demonstrated (*The Courtly Maker*) that often the 'rhythm supplies the meaning', and the 'structure of the poem is directly related to what it is "about"'. Wyatt constantly exploits 'the "broken-backed" line which consists of two balancing phrases'. This, of course, is something he inherits from an earlier tradition; so, too, is his use of alliteration. Even when it is obvious, it is handled musically: 'Lux, my fair falcon, and your fellows all . . . Ye not forsake me that fair might ye befall' [17]. He also frequently uses it lightly and with great delicacy, as in 'To make an end of all this strife' [60]. In the Satires, as in the opening of 'Mine own John Poyntz' [64], it is used to add emphasis.

Wyatt's rhythmical skill is further shown in the way he combines his conversational style with the musical quality of his lyrics. This is obvious in such poems as 'All heavy minds' [20], 'What means this' [27], 'Is it possible?' [36], 'And wilt thou leave me thus?' [33], 'Forget not yet' [57], and 'Ye know my heart' [53] with its complicated structure and intricate rhyme scheme. Four of these lyrics have a refrain, a device that Wyatt frequently uses and which suggests that they were meant to be sung. He sometimes also takes the last shorter line of a stanza and uses it as the opening phrase of the next stanza. This is handled especially

14

well in 'Such hap as I am happèd in' [55] and 'To make an end of all this strife' [60].

'At most mischief' [44], with its two-stressed line and repetitive rhyming, and 'Longer to muse' [46], suggest a certain inheritance from Skelton. They also demonstrate Wyatt's rhythmical skill with short lines that again use everyday words. Both poems are surely lyrics to be sung.

'At most mischief' is among a number of poems, including the famous 'My lute, awake!' [18], in which Wyatt refers to his lute and from which, presumably, it has been assumed that he played the instrument. John Stevens, however, in his excellent book, *Music and Poetry in the Early Tudor Court*, maintains that 'there is no evidence whatsoever that he (Wyatt) had musical ability, as singer, lutenist or composer'. Stevens even suggests that Wyatt's poetry confirms his lack of interest in music, and he points out that there is only one surviving musical setting of a poem by Wyatt, namely, Cornish's setting of 'Ah, Robin' [22]. Lute tablatures for some others 'are dated about 1550 or later'. Yet he does concede that 'Courtly education would certainly have laid some stress on practical music' and that a courtier such as Wyatt would have 'learnt to sing a little and strum upon the lute'.

Bearing in mind the revival of music at the Court of Henry VIII, and the nature of Wyatt's lyrics, surely this is all that is needed. It is known that many songs were sung to already popular tunes and that music was improvised. Wyatt may have done no more than many present-day pop-singers, who manage to get by having learnt only a few chords for the guitar. Whether Wyatt played the lute or merely strummed upon it, what surely cannot be denied is that the quality of many of the lyrics suggest that they were meant to be sung. Nevertheless, most of them can stand on their own as poems to be read. So it is not wholly fair to regard Wyatt's courtly love lyrics as comparable with other post-Chaucer lyrics as mere gambits in the 'game of love'. We have already seen how Wyatt used this convention to express both his personal emotions and the beliefs and values that were important to him. He is dealing with the world in which he lives, with all its

15

uncertainties and hazards and the insecurity it generates in his own mind. This is not typical of other lyrics of courtly love, and it is one of the reasons why Wyatt is a far greater poet than any of the others between Chaucer and at least his own time.

Wyatt was only too aware that the love implied in the poems of courtly love was both insubstantial and hypocritical, although in none of them does he accuse the convention itself of hypocrisy. He needed something far more secure, and seemingly he found it in his last five years (until Henry forced him back to his wife) in the love of Elizabeth Darrell, who was formerly one of Catherine of Aragon's maids of honour.

It was for Catherine of Aragon that Wyatt translated Plutarch's essay 'Quyete of Mynde', and it is possible to see all Wyatt's poetry from the sonnets, through the love lyrics to the satires and psalms, as a quest for the quiet mind. He refers to it in the sonnet, 'Ever mine hap' [11], in which he makes full use of paradox to emphasize how impossible it is to find peace or quietness of mind in his love. The 'snow shall be black', the 'sea waterless', and there will be 'fish in the mountain', before he finds such 'peace or quietness'.

It is the Satires and the Psalms which suggest that possible sources for the peace and quiet he needs are to be found in the natural life of the countryside and in his Christian faith.

The one quality that characterizes all three satires – apart from bitterness and their ironic critique of Court life – is an essential honesty. They were almost certainly written in 1536-7, after his release from the Tower and before he went to Spain. The first [64] is addressed to his friend and fellow courtier, John Poyntz. While he fairly admits that he is not untouched by the 'glory and fire' of Court life, he cannot abide the hypocrisy: 'Use wiles for wit and make deceit a pleasure'. In spite of his unquestioned loyalty to his king, his honesty forces him to declare that he won't accept 'tyranny/To be the right of a prince's reign./I cannot I; no, no, it will not be!' He prefers the life of a country gentleman. He is critical of France and Spain, and of Rome, 'where Christ is given in prey/For money, poison and treason'.

The second satire (not in this selection) emphasizes the desirability of the natural, private life in contrast to courtly ambition, and, in the third satire [65], as A.K. Foxwell says, 'he strikes deeper. It is not only the want of truth in the world but the assumption of truth by the false-hearted in an outward show of morality that does most harm.' Ironically, he advises his fellow courtier and poet, Sir Francis Bryan, to flee from truth and even to prostitute his close relatives if needs be in the pursuit of wealth. Thus the poem attacks selfishness and greed and, since Bryan declines to behave hypocritically, is a plea for moral integrity.

The first satire derives from Alamanni and the third from Horace, but they are essentially original works deserving of Kenneth Muir's judgement that Wyatt 'was the first English writer of formal satire'. Skelton had almost done it earlier in his play 'Magnificence' and the poems 'Speak Parrot' and 'Colin Clout', but Skelton was altogether more savage and vituperative in his attacks upon the Court, all clerics in general and Wolsey in particular. Wyatt is witty yet more urbane and considered, justifying the epithet 'formal', a style which Dryden and Pope were to develop.

Technically, the satires are innovative. They use Alamanni's *terza rima* but with greater fluidity, Wyatt's thought flowing not only from line to line but from one tercet to another. At times he is almost writing blank verse, and his handling of enjambment foreshadows the later development of free verse. He makes pertinent use of proverbs, as he does in many poems, and the conversational tone of everyday speech is employed with great effect, his ear being as sensitive as ever in his use of rhyme and rhythm.

Terza rima is also used for his paraphrase of the penitential psalms, and Southall considers that Wyatt's use of enjambment in these poems is not 'matched until Shakespeare'. There are seven penitential psalms (numbers 6, 32, 38, 51, 102, 130 and 143) each with a narrative prologue dealing with the nature and state of mind of David as their author. This gives to the whole series the character of one long poem. I have chosen Psalms 102 and 130

17

because they seem to me more original, in that Wyatt departs more freely from his sources. These, primarily, were paraphrases by Pietro Aretino and Joannis Campensis, Latin translations by Ulrich Zwingli, an English translation of Zwingli by George Joye, the Latin Vulgate, and perhaps the Coverdale Bible of 1535. It is not known when the paraphrases were written. Scholars have argued for both 1536 and 1541. The safest assumption would seem to be sometime between those two dates.

Wyatt's last and fatal diplomatic task ended his quest for the quiet mind, and we are left with the psychological drama of the poems. They, at any rate, establish him not only as a skilled craftsman and a pioneer in new forms of verse, but as a man who sought to resolve the conflicting emotions that beset his insecure life in a personal poetry that was in advance of his time and resulted in some of the finest lyrics in the English language.

Textual Note and Select Bibliography

I have tried to select what seem to me to be the best of Wyatt's poems and, at the same time, to provide a selection that well represents his skill in a variety of verse forms. Thus, among these 67 poems, there are, if one counts differing rhyming schemes, about 40 different kinds of stanza.

No attempt has been made to use the poems chronologically; instead, I have been more concerned to arrange them so as to accommodate as many as possible in the available space. Spelling has been modernized. Archaic words have been retained only when to alter them would seriously alter the rhythm. The meaning of such words can be found in the Notes.

Among the various editors there is no unanimity about punctuation, and I don't see how there could be. Much of the punctuation in Wyatt's poems has been provided by scribes and others, except, presumably, in the poems in Wyatt's own hand in the Egerton MS. Many poems have no punctuation at all. In others

18

it is used lightly and, as Southall says, 'principally as a rhythmical device...to mark the pauses arising from the "voice" of the poem, and only secondarily to indicate its grammatical construction.' Wyatt's main marks are the full stop and the virgule (/). I have tried to achieve a balance between Wyatt's rhythmical intentions and intelligibility for the modern reader. So I have sometimes tended to use the comma as Wyatt might have used the virgule, to indicate a phrasal pause.

Apart from the odd sonnet or lyric of doubtful authenticity and published anonymously in the anthology *The Court of Venus*, none of Wyatt's poems were published in his lifetime. A number appeared in *Songes and Sonettes written by the ryght honorable Lorde Henry Howard, Late Earle of Surrey, and other*, published by Richard Tottel in 1557, and now usually referred to as *Tottel's Miscellany*. Unfortunately, the editors thought they could improve some of Wyatt's poems by making them comply with the fashionable verse of the time written in regular metres.

His poems are contained in a number of manuscripts. The most important is the Egerton MS [E]. It has more than a hundred of Wyatt's lyrics, the satires and psalms. Most of the later poems are in Wyatt's own hand, and several others have corrections and revisions by him. Other MSS include the Devonshire MS [D] which has, among the poems attributed to Wyatt, earlier versions of some of the poems in E; the Blage MS [B], probably compiled by Wyatt's friend, Sir George Blage, and the Arundel MS [A], which has some 40 poems that are in other MSS.

In determining the texts for this selection, I am especially indebted to *The Works of Henry Howard, Earl of Surrey and Sir Thomas Wyatt the Elder*, ed. G. Nott (2 vols, London, 1815-16); *The Poems of Sir Thomas Wiat*, ed. A.K. Foxwell (2 vols, University of London Press, 1913) [Fx]; *The Poetry of Sir Thomas Wyatt*, E.M.W. Tillyard (Chatto & Windus, 1949); *Collected Poems of Sir Thomas Wyatt*, ed. Kenneth Muir and Patricia Thomson (Liverpool University Press, 1969) [M&T]; *Sir Thomas Wyatt: Collected Poems*, ed. Joost Daalder (Oxford University Press, 1975), and *Sir Thomas Wyatt: The Complete Poems*, ed. R.A. Rebholz (Penguin, 1978).

From a large bibliography, I have also found the following publications especially important: *Sir Thomas Wyatt*, Sergio Baldi, trans. F.T. Prince (Longman, 1961); *Sir Thomas Wyatt and some Collected Studies*, E.K. Chambers (Sidgwick & Jackson, 1933); *Humanism and Poetry in the Early Tudor Period*, H.A. Mason (Routledge & Kegan Paul, 1959); *Editing Wyatt*, H.A. Mason (*Cambridge Quarterly*, 1972); *The Life and Letters of Sir Thomas Wyatt*, Kenneth Muir (Liverpool University Press, 1963); *The Courtly Maker*, Raymond Southall (Basil Blackwell, 1964); *Music and Poetry in the Early Tudor Court*, John Stevens (Cambridge University Press, 1961); *Sir Thomas Wyatt and His Background*, Patricia Thomson (Routledge & Kegan Paul, 1964), and *Wyatt: The Critical Heritage*, ed. Patricia Thomson (Routledge & Kegan Paul, 1974).

Sonnets

1

Whoso list to hunt, I know where is an hind,
But as for me, alas, I may no more.
The vain travail hath wearied me so sore,
I am of them that farthest cometh behind,
Yet may I by no means my wearied mind
Draw from the deer, but as she fleeth afore
Fainting I follow. I leave off therefore
Since in a net I seek to hold the wind.
Who list her hunt, I put him out of doubt,
As well as I may spend his time in vain,   10
And graven with diamonds in letters plain
There is written her fair neck round about:
'*Noli me tangere* for Caesar's I am,
And wild for to hold though I seem tame.'

2

I find no peace, and all my war is done,
I fear and hope, I burn and freeze like ice,
I fly above the wind, yet can I not arise,
And naught I have, and all the world I season.
That looseth nor locketh, holdeth me in prison,
And holdeth me not, yet can I scape no wise,
Nor letteth me live, nor die at my device,
And yet of death it giveth me occasion.
Without eyen I see, and without tongue I plain,
I desire to perish, and yet I ask health,   10
I love another, and thus I hate myself,
I feed me in sorrow, and laugh in all my pain,
Likewise displeaseth me both death and life,
And my delight is causer of this strife.

3

My galley chargèd with forgetfulness
Thorough sharp seas in winter nights doth pass
'Tween rock and rock; and eke mine enemy, alas,
That is my lord, steereth with cruelness,
And every oar a thought in readiness,
As though that death were light in such a case.
An endless wind doth tear the sail apace,
Of forced sighs and trusty fearfulness.
A rain of tears, a cloud of dark disdain
Hath done the wearied cords great hindrance,   10
Wreathed with error, and eke with ignorance,
The stars be hid that led me to this pain,
Drownèd is reason that should me comfort,
And I remain despairing of the port.

4

Unstable dream, according to the place,
Be steadfast once, or else at least be true.
By tasted sweetness make me not to rue
The sudden loss of thy false feignèd grace.
By good respect, in such a dangerous case,
Thou brought'st not her into this tossing mew,
But madest my sprite live my care to renew,
My body in tempest, her succour to embrace.
The body dead, the sprite had his desire,
Painless was the one, the other in delight.   10
Why then, alas, did it not keep it right,
Returning to leap into the fire,
And where it was at wish it could not remain?
Such mocks of dreams they turn to deadly pain.

5

If waker care, if sudden pale colour,
If many sighs, with little speech to plain,
Now joy, now woe, if they my cheer disdain,
For hope of small, if much to fear therefore,
To haste, to slack my pace less or more,
Be sign of love, then do I love again.
If thou ask whom, sure since I did refrain
Brunet that set my wealth in such a roar,
Th'unfeignèd cheer of Phyllis hath the place
That Brunet had. She hath and ever shall.   10
She from myself now hath me in her grace.
She hath in hand my wit, my will, and all.
My heart alone well worthy she doth stay,
Without whose help scant do I live a day.

6

The pillar perished is whereto I leant,
The strongest stay of mine unquiet mind.
The like of it no man again can find
From east to west, still seeking though he went.
To mine unhap, for hap away hath rent
Of all my joy the very bark and rind,
And I, alas, by chance am thus assigned
Dearly to mourn, till death do it relent.
But since that thus it is by destiny,
What can I more but have a woeful heart,   10
My pen in plaint, my voice in woeful cry,
My mind in woe, my body full of smart,
And I myself, myself always to hate
Till dreadful death, do cease my doeful state.

7

You that in love find luck and abundance,
And live in lust and joyful jollity,
Arise, for shame, do away your sluggardy,
Arise, I say, do May some observance!
Let me in bed lie dreaming in mischance,
Let me remember the haps most unhappy
That me betide in May most commonly,
As one whom love list little to advance.
Sephame said true that my nativity
Mischanced was with the ruler of the May.   10
He guessed, I prove of that the verity,
In May my wealth and eke my life, I say,
Have stood so oft in such perplexity.
Rejoice! Let me dream of your felicity.

8

My love took scorn my service to retain,
Wherein me thought she usèd cruelty,
Since with good will I lost my liberty
To follow her, which causeth all my pain.
Might never care cause me for to refrain,
But only this, which is extremity,
Giving me naught, alas, not to agree
That as I was her man I might remain.
But since that thus ye list to order me
That would have been your servant true and fast,   10
Displease thee not, my doting days be past,
And with my loss to live I must agree.
For as there is a certain time to rage,
So is there time such madness to assuage.

9

The flaming sighs that boil within my breast
Sometime break forth, and they can well declare
The heart's unrest and how that it doth fare,
The pain thereof, the grief, and all the rest.
The watered eyes from whence the tears do fall
Do feel some force, or else they would be dry;
The wasted flesh of colour dead can try,
And something tell what sweetness is in gall.
And he that list to see and to discern
How care can force within a wearied mind,   10
Come he to me: I am that place assigned.
But for all this no force, it doth no harm.
The wound, alas, hap in some other place,
From whence no tool away the scar can raze.

But you that of such like have had your part
Can best be judge. Wherefore, my friend so dear,
I thought it good my state should now appear
To you, and that there is no great desert.
And whereas you, in weighty matters great,
Of fortune saw the shadow that you know,   20
For trifling things I now am stricken so
That, though I feel my heart doth wound and beat,
I sit alone, save on the second day
My fever comes, with whom I spend the time
In burning heat, while that she list assign.
And who hath health and liberty alway,
Let him thank God, and let him not provoke
To have the like of this my painful stroke.

10

I abide and abide and better abide,
And after the old proverb, the happy day,
And ever my lady to me doth say,
'Let me alone and I will provide.'
I abide and abide and tarry the tide,
And with abiding speed well ye may.
Thus do I abide, I wot, alway,
Neither obtaining nor yet denied.
Aye me, this long abiding
Seemeth to me, as who sayeth,   10
A prolonging of a dying death,
Or a refusing of a desired thing.
Much were it better for to be plain
Than to say 'Abide', and yet shall not obtain.

11

Ever mine hap is slack and slow in coming,
Desire increasing, mine hope uncertain,
That leave it or wait it doth me like pain,
And tiger-like swift it is in parting.
Alas, the snow shall be black and scalding,
The sea waterless, fish in the mountain,
The Thames shall return back into his fountain,
And where he rose the sun shall take lodging,
Ere that I in this find peace or quietness,
In that Love or my lady rightwisely   10
Leave to conspire again me wrongfully.
And if that I have after such bitterness
Anything sweet, my mouth is out of taste,
That all my trust and travail is but waste.

Epigrams

12

Who hath heard of such cruelty before?
That when my plaint remembered her my woe
That caused it, she cruel more and more,
Wished each stitch, as she did sit and sew,
Had pricked mine heart, for to increase my sore.
And, as I think, she thought it had been so,
For as she thought, 'This is his heart indeed,'
She pricked hard, and made herself to bleed.

13

Th'en'my of life, decayer of all kind,
That with his cold withers away the green,
This other night me in my bed did find,
And offered me to rid my fever clean; .
And I did grant, so did despair me blind.
He drew his bow with arrow sharp and keen,
And struck the place where love had hit before,
And drove the first dart deeper more and more.

14

Tagus, farewell, that westward with thy streams
Turns up the grains of gold already tried,
With spur and sail for I go seek the Thames,
Gainward the sun that show'th her wealthy pride
And, to the town which Brutus sought by dreams,
Like bended moon doth lend her lusty side.
My king, my country, alone for whom I live,
Of mighty love the wings for this me give.

15

Sighs are my food, drink are my tears,
Clinking of fetters such music would crave.
Stink and close air away my life wears,
Innocency is all the hope I have.
Rain, wind, or weather I judge by mine ears.
Malice assaulted that righteousness should save.
Sure I am, Bryan, this wound shall heal again,
But yet, alas, the scar shall still remain.

16

A face that should content me wondrous well
Should not be fair but comely to behold,
With gladsome look all grief for to expel,
With sober cheer so would I that it should
Speak without words, such words that none can tell.
The tress also should be of crispèd gold.
With wit and these might chance I might be tied,
And knit again the knot that should not slide.

17

Lux, my fair falcon, and your fellows all,
How well pleasant it were your liberty!
Ye not forsake me that fair might ye befall,
But they that sometime liked my company
Like lice away from dead bodies they crawl.
Lo, what a proof in light adversity!
But ye, my birds, I swear by all your bells,
Ye be my friends, and so be but few else.

Songs and Lyrics

18

My lute, awake! Perform the last
Labour that thou and I shall waste,
And end that I have now begun,
For when this song is sung and past,
My lute be still, for I have done.

As to be heard where ear is none,
As lead to grave in marble stone,
My song may pierce her heart as soon.
. Should we then sigh or sing or moan?
No, no, my lute, for I have done. 10

The rocks do not so cruelly
Repulse the waves continually
As she my suit and affection,
So that I am past remedy,
Whereby my lute and I have done.

Proud of the spoil that thou hast got
Of simple hearts thorough love's shot,
By whom, unkind, thou hast them won,
Think not he has his bow forgot,
Although my lute and I have done. 20

Vengeance shall fall on thy disdain
That mak'st but game on earnest pain.
Think not alone under the sun
Unquit to cause thy lovers plain,
Although my lute and I have done.

May chance thee lie withered and old
The winter nights that are so cold,
Plaining in vain unto the moon.
Thy wishes then dare not be told.
Care then who list, for I have done.   30

And then may chance thee to repent
The time that thou hast lost and spent
To cause thy lovers sigh and swoon.
Then shalt thou know beauty but lent,
And wish and want as I have done.

Now cease, my lute. This is the last
Labour that thou and I shall waste,
And ended is that we begun.
Now is this song both sung and past.
My lute, be still, for I have done.   40

19
Blame not my lute, for he must sound
Of this or that as liketh me;
For lack of wit the lute is bound
To give such tunes as pleaseth me.
Though my songs be somewhat strange
And speak such words as touch thy change,
    Blame not my lute.

My lute, alas, doth not offend,
Though that perforce he must agree
To sound such tunes as I intend,   10
To sing to them that heareth me.
Then though my songs be somewhat plain
And toucheth some that use to feign,
    Blame not my lute.

My lute and strings may not deny,
But as I strike they must obey.
Break not them then so wrongfully,
But wreak thyself some wiser way;
And though the songs which I indite
Do quit thy change with rightful spite,   20
     Blame not my lute.

Spite asketh spite, and changing change,
And falsèd faith must needs be known;
The faults so great, the case so strange,
Of right it must abroad be blown.
Then since that by thine own desert
My songs do tell how true thou art,
     Blame not my lute.

Blame but thyself that hast misdone,
And well deservèd to have blame;   30
Change thou thy way so evil begun,
And then my lute shall sound that same.
But if till then my fingers play
By thy desert their wonted way,
     Blame not my lute.

Farewell, unknown, for though thou break
My strings in spite with great disdain,
Yet have I found out for thy sake
Strings for to string my lute again.
And if perchance this foolish rhyme   40
Do make thee blush at any time,
     Blame not my lute.

20
　　All heavy minds
Do seek to ease their charge,
And that that most them binds
　　To let at large.

　　Then why should I
Hold pain within my heart,
And may my tune apply
　　To ease my smart?

　　My faithful lute
Alone shall hear me plain,　　　　　　　　　10
For else all other suit
　　Is clean in vain.

　　For where I sue
Redress of all my grief,
Lo, they do most eschew
　　My heart's relief.

　　Alas, my dear,
Have I deserved so
That no help may appear
　　Of all my woe?　　　　　　　　　　　　20

　　Whom speak I to,
Unkind and deaf of ear?
Alas, lo, I go,
　　And wot not where.

　　Where is my thought?
Where wanders my desire?
Where may the thing be sought
　　That I require?

Light in the wind
Doth flee all my delight,
Where truth and faithful mind
    Are put to flight.   30

Who shall me give
Feathered wings for to flee
The thing that doth me grieve
    That I may see?

Who would go seek
The cause whereby to plain?
Who would his foe beseek
    For ease of pain?   40

My chance doth so
My woeful case procure,
To offer to my foe
    My heart to cure.

What hope I then
To have any redress?
Of whom, or where, or when,
    Who can express?

No, since despair
Hath set me in this case,   50
In vain oft in the air
    To say 'Alas!'

I seek nothing
But thus for to discharge
My heart of sore sighing,
    To plain at large,

And with my lute
Sometime to ease my pain,
For else all other suit
    Is clean in vain.   60

21

In eternum I was once determed
For to have loved, and my mind affirmed
That with my heart it should be confirmed
    In eternum.

Forthwith I found the thing that I might like,
And sought with love to warm her heart alike,
For as me thought I should not see the like
    In eternum.

To trace this dance I put myself in press.
Vain hope did lead and bade I should not cease   10
To serve, to suffer, and still to hold my peace
    In eternum.

With this first rule I furthered me apace
That, as methought, my troth had taken place
With full assurance to stand in her grace
    In eternum.

It was not long ere I by proof had found
That feeble building is on feeble ground,
For in her heart this word did never sound,
    In eternum.   20

In eternum then from my heart I cast
That I had first determined for the best.
Now in the place another thought doth rest
    In eternum.

22

'Ah, Robin,
Jolly Robin,
Tell me how thy leman doth,
And thou shall know of mine.'

'My lady is unkind, perdie!'
   'Alack, why is she so?'
'She loveth another better than me,
   And yet she will say no.'

Response: I find no such doubleness,
      I find women true.   10
   My lady loveth me doubtless,
      And will change for no new.

Le Plaintif: Thou art happy while that doth last,
      But I say as I find,
   That women's love is but a blast,
      And turneth like the wind.

Response: If that be true yet as thou say'st
      That women turn their heart,
   Then speak better of them thou mayst,
      In hope to have thy part.   20

Le Plaintif: Such folks shall take no harm by love
      That can abide their turn,
   But I, alas, can no way prove
      In love but lack and mourn.

Response: But if thou wilt avoid thy harm,
      Learn this lesson of me:
   At others' fires thyself to warm,
      And let them warm with thee.

23

O goodly hand
Wherein doth stand
My heart distressed in pain,
Fair hand, alas,
In little space
My life that doth restrain.

O fingers slight,
Departed right,
So long, so small, so round,
Goodly begone,   10
And yet alone
Most cruel in my wound.

With lilies white
And roses bright
Doth strive thy colour fair;
Nature did lend
Each finger's end
A pearl for to repair.

Consent at last,
Since that thou hast   20
My heart in thy demesne,
For service true
On me to rue,
And reach me love again.

And if not so,
Then with more woe
Enforce thyself to strain
This simple heart,
That suffereth smart,
And rid it out of pain.   30

24

Perdie, I said it not
Nor never thought to do.
As well as I, ye wot
I have no power thereto.
And if I did, the lot
That first did me enchain
Do never slack the knot,
But straiter to my pain.

And if I did, each thing
That may do harm or woe   10
Continually may wring
My heart whereso I go.
Report may always ring
Of shame of me for ay,
If in my heart did spring
The word that ye do say.

If I said so, each star
That is in heaven above
May frown on me to mar
The hope I have in love.   20
And if I did, such war
As they brought out of Troy
Bring all my life afar
From all this lust and joy.

And if I did so say,
The beauty that me bound
Increase from day to day
More cruel to my wound.
With all the moan that may,
To plaint may turn my song.   30
My life may soon decay,
Without redress, by wrong.

If I be clear fro thought,
Why do ye then complain?
Then is this thing but sought
To turn me to more pain.
Then that that ye have wrought
Ye must it now redress.
Of right therefore ye ought
Such rigour to repress.   40

And as I have deserved,
So grant me now my hire.
Ye know I never swerved,
Ye never found me liar.
For Rachel have I served,
(For Leah care I never)
And her I have reserved
Within my heart for ever.

25
Madam, withouten many words,
Once, I am sure, ye will or no:
And if ye will, then leave your bourds,
And use your wit, and show it so.

And with a beck ye shall me call,
And if of one that burneth alway
Ye have any pity at all,
Answer him fair with yea or nay.

If it be yea, I shall be fain;
If it be nay, friends as before.   10
Ye shall another man obtain,
And I mine own, and yours no more.

26

Patience, though I have not
The thing that I require,
I must of force, God wot,
Forbear my most desire,
For no ways can I find
To sail against the wind.

Patience, do what they will
To work me woe or spite,
I shall content me still
To think both day and night,   10
To think and hold my peace
Since there is no redress.

Patience, withouten blame,
For I offended nought.
I know they know the same,
Though they have changed their thought.
Was ever thought so moved
To hate that it hath loved?

Patience of all my harm,
For Fortune is my foe;   20
Patience must be the charm
To heal me of my woe.
Patience without offence
Is a painful patience.

27

What means this? When I lie alone
I toss, I turn, I sigh, I groan.
My bed me seems as hard as stone:
        What means this?

I sigh, I plain continually,
The clothes that on my bed do lie
Always me think they lie awry:
 What means this?

In slumbers oft for fear I quake,
For heat and cold I burn and shake,
For lack of sleep my head doth ache:
 What means this?

A mornings then when I do rise,
I turn unto my wonted guise,
All day after muse and devise:
 What means this?

And if perchance by me there pass
She unto whom I sue for grace,
The cold blood forsaketh my face:
 What means this?

But if I sit near her by,
With loud voice my heart doth cry,
And yet my mouth is dumb and dry:
 What means this?

To ask for help no heart I have,
My tongue doth fail what I should crave,
Yet inwardly I rage and rave:
 What means this?

Thus have I passed many a year,
And many a day, though naught appear
But most of that that most I fear:
 What means this?

10

20

30

But I see well that your high disdain
Will no wise grant that I shall more attain;
Yet ye must grant at the least
This my poor and small request:
    Rejoice not at my pain.   20

33
   And wilt thou leave me thus?
   Say nay, say nay, for shame,
   To save thee from the blame
   Of all my grief and grame.
   And wilt thou leave me thus?
      Say nay, say nay.

   And wilt thou leave me thus,
   That hath loved thee so long,
   In wealth and woe among?
   And is thy heart so strong   10
   As for to leave me thus?
      Say nay, say nay.

   And wilt thou leave me thus,
   That hath given thee my heart
   Never for to depart,
   Neither for pain nor smart?
   And wilt thou leave me thus?
      Say nay, say nay.

   And wilt thou leave me thus,
   And have no more pity   20
   Of him that loveth thee?
   Alas, thy cruelty!
   And wilt thou leave me thus?
      Say nay, say nay.

34

Since you will needs that I shall sing,
Take it in worth such as I have,
Plenty of plaint, moan, and mourning,
In deep despair and deadly pain,
Bootless for boot, crying to crave,
    To crave in vain.

Such hammers work within my head,
That sound naught else unto my ears
But fast at board and wake abed:
Such tune the temper to my song   10
To wail my wrong, that I want tears
    To wail my wrong.

Death and despair afore my face,
My days decay, my grief doth grow.
The cause thereof is in this place,
Whom cruelty doth still constrain
For to rejoice, though it be woe
    To hear me plain.

A broken lute, untuned strings
With such a song may well bear part,   20
That neither pleases him that sings
Nor them that hear, but her alone,
That with her heart would strain my heart
    To hear it groan.

If it grieve you to hear this same
That you do feel but in my voice,
Consider then what pleasant game
I do sustain in every part,
To cause me sing or to rejoice
    Within my heart.   30

35

There was never nothing more me pained,
    Nor nothing more me moved,
As when my sweetheart her complained
    That ever she me loved.
        Alas the while!

With piteous look she said and sighed:
    'Alas what aileth me,
To love and set my wealth so light
    On him that loveth not me?
        Alas the while!   10

'Was I not well void of all my pain,
    When that nothing me grieved?
And now with sorrows I must complain
    And cannot be relieved,
        Alas the while!

'My restful nights and joyful days,
    Since I began to love,
Be take from me. All thing decays,
    Yet can I not remove.
        Alas the while!'   20

She wept and wrung her hands withal,
    The tears fell in my neck.
She turned her face and let it fall,
    Scarcely therewith could speak.
        Alas the while!

Her pains tormented me so sore
    That comfort had I none,
But cursed my fortune more and more
    To see her sob and groan.
        Alas the while!   30

36
Is it possible
That so high debate
So sharp, so sore, and of such rate,
Should end so soon and was begun so late?
Is it possible?

Is it possible
So cruel intent,
So hasty heat, and so soon spent,
From love to hate, and thence for to relent?
Is it possible?   10

Is it possible
That any may find
Within one heart so diverse mind,
To change or turn as weather and wind?
Is it possible?

Is it possible
To spy it in an eye
That turns as oft as chance on die,
The truth whereof can any try?
Is it possible?   20

It is possible
For to turn so oft,
To bring that lowest that was most aloft,
And to fall highest yet to light soft.
It is possible.

All is possible,
Whoso list believe.
Trust therefore first, and after preve,
As men wed ladies by licence and leave,
All is possible.   30

37

Marvel no more although
The songs I sing do moan,
For other life than woe
I never proved none;
And in my heart also
Is graven with letters deep
A thousand sighs and moe,
A flood of tears to weep.

How may a man in smart
Find matter to rejoice?   10
How may a mourning heart
Set forth a pleasant voice?
Play who that can the part,
Needs must in me appear
How fortune overthwart
Doth cause my mourning cheer.

Perdie, there is no man,
If he never saw sight,
That perfectly tell can
The nature of the light.   20
Alas, how should I then,
That never tasted but sour,
But do as I began,
Continually to lour?

But yet perchance some chance
May chance to change my tune,
And when such chance doth chance
Then shall I thank Fortune;
And if I have such chance,
Perchance ere it be long,   30
For such a pleasant chance
To sing some pleasant song.

38
Tangled I was in love's snare,
Oppressed with pain, torment with care,
Of grief right sure, of joy full bare,
Clean in despair by cruelty.
But ha, ha, ha, full well is me,
For I am now at liberty.

The woeful days so full of pain,
The weary night all spent in vain,
The labour lost for no small gain,
To write them all it will not be.   10
But ha, ha, ha, full well is me,
For I am now at liberty.

Everything that fair doth show,
When proof is made it proveth not so,
But turneth mirth to bitter woe,
Which in this case full well I see.
But ha, ha, ha, full well is me,
For I am now at liberty.

Too great desire was my guide,
And wanton will went by my side;   20
Hope rulèd still and made me bide
Of love's craft the extremity.
But ha, ha, ha, full well is me,
For I am now at liberty.

With feignèd words, which were but wind,
Too long delays I was assigned;
Her wily looks my wits did blind,
Thus as she would I did agree.
But ha, ha, ha, full well is me,
For I am now at liberty.   30

Was never bird tangled in lime
That brake away in better time
Than I that rotten boughs did climb
And had no hurt, but scapèd free.
Now ha, ha, ha, full well is me,
For I am now at liberty.

39
When first mine eyes did view and mark
Thy fair beauty to behold,
And when mine ears listened to hark
The pleasant words that thou me told,
I would as then I had been free
From ears to hear and eyes to see.

And when my lips gan first to move,
Whereby my heart to thee was known,
And when my tongue did talk of love
To thee that has true love down thrown,   10
I would my lips and tongue also
Had then been dumb, no deal to go.

And when my hands have handled aught
That thee hath kept in memory,
And when my feet have gone and sought
To find and get thy company,
I would each hand a foot had been,
And I each foot a hand had seen.

And when in mind I did consent
To follow this my fancy's will,   20
And when my heart did first relent
To taste such bait my life to spill,
I would mine heart had been as thine,
Or else thy heart had been as mine.

40

To wish and want and not obtain,
To seek and sue ease of my pain,
Since all that ever I do is vain,
    What may it avail me?

Although I strive both day and hour
Against the stream with all my power,
If fortune list yet for to lour,
    What may it avail me?

If willingly I suffer woe,
If from the fire me list not go,   10
If then I burn to plain me so,
    What may it avail me?

And if the harm that I suffer
Be run too far out of measure,
To seek for help any further,
    What may it avail me?

What though each heart that heareth me plain,
Pitieth and plaineth for my pain,
If I no less in grief remain,
    What may it avail me?   20

Yea, though the want of my relief
Displease the causer of my grief,
Since I remain still in mischief,
    What may it avail me?

Such cruel chance doth so me threat,
Continually inward to fret,
Then of release for to entreat
    What may it avail me?

Fortune is deaf unto my call,
My torment moveth her not at all, 30
And though she turn as doth a ball,
  What may it avail me?

For in despair there is no rede;
To want of ear speech is no speed;
To linger still, alive as dead,
  What may it avail me?

41
It may be good, like it who list,
But I do doubt. Who can blame me?
For oft assured yet have I missed,
And now again I fear the same.
The windy words, the eyes' quaint game,
Of sudden change maketh me aghast:
For dread to fall I stand not fast.

Alas, I tread an endless maze
That seek to accord two contraries,
And hope still, and nothing hase, 10
Imprisoned in liberties,
As one unheard, and still that cries,
Always thirsty, yet naught I taste:
For dread to fall I stand not fast.

Assured I doubt I be not sure;
And should I trust to such surety
That oft hath put the proof in ure,
And never hath found it trusty?
Nay, sir, in faith it were great folly.
And yet my life thus I do waste, 20
For dread to fall I stand not fast.

42

My hope, alas, hath me abused,
And vain rejoicing hath me fed;
Lust and joy have me refused,
And careful plaint is in their stead.
Too much advancing slacked my speed,
Mirth hath caused my heaviness,
And I remain all comfortless.

Whereto did I assure my thought
Without displeasure steadfastly?
In Fortune's forge my joy was wrought,   10
And is revolted readily.
I am mistaken wonderly,
For I thought naught but faithfulness,
Yet I remain all comfortless.

In gladsome cheer I did delight,
Till that delight did cause my smart,
And all was wrong where I thought right;
For right it was that my true heart
Should not from truth be set apart,
Since truth did cause my hardiness: 20
Yet I remain all comfortless.

Sometime delight did tune my song,
And led my heart full pleasantly,
And to myself I said among,
My hap is coming hastily.
But it hath happed contrary:
Assurance caused my distress,
And I remain all comfortless.

Then if my note now do vary,
And leave his wonted pleasantness,   30
The heavy burden that I carry
Hath altered all my joyfulness.
No pleasure hath still steadfastness,
But haste hath hurt my happiness,
And I remain all comfortless.

43

What rage is this? What furor of what kind?
What pow'r, what plague doth weary thus my mind?
Within my bones to rankle is assigned
    What poison, pleasant sweet?

Lo, see mine eyes swell with continual tears,
The body still away sleepless it wears,
My food nothing my fainting strength repairs,
    Nor doth my limbs sustain.

In deep wide wound the deadly stroke doth turn,
To curèd scar that never shall return.   10
Go to, triumph, rejoice thy goodly turn,
    Thy friend thou dost oppress.

Oppress thou dost, and hast of him no cure,
Nor yet my plaint no pity can procure.
Fierce tiger fell, hard rock without recure,
    Cruel rebel to love.

Once may thou love, never be loved again,
So love thou still, and not thy love obtain.
So wrathful love, with spites of just disdain
    May threat thy cruel heart.   20

44

At most mischief
I suffer grief,
For of relief
Since I have none,
My lute and I
Continually
Shall us apply
To sigh and moan.

Naught may prevail
To weep or wail. 10
Pity doth fail
In you, alas.
Mourning or moan,
Complaint or none,
It is all one
As in this case.

For cruelty
Most that can be
Hath sovereignty
Within your heart, 20
Which maketh bare
All my welfare:
Naught do ye care
How sore I smart.

No tiger's heart
Is so pervert
Without desert
To wreak his ire.
And you me kill
For my goodwill, 30
Lo how I spill
For my desire.

There is no love
That can ye move,
And I can prove
None other way.
Therefore I must
Restrain my lust,
Banish my trust
And wealth away.   40

Thus in mischief
I suffer grief,
For of relief,
Since I have none,
My lute and I
Continually
Shall us apply
To sigh and moan.

45

If with complaint the pain might be expressed,
That inwardly doth cause me sigh and groan,
    Your hard heart and your cruel breast
    Should sigh and plain for my unrest;
        And though it were of stone,
Yet should remorse cause it relent and moan.

But since it is so far out of measure,
That with my words I can it not contain,
    My only trust, my heart's treasure,
    Alas, why do I still endure   10
        This restless smart and pain,
Since if ye list, ye may my woe restrain?

46

> Longer to muse
> On this refuse
> I will not use,
> But study to forget;
> Letting all go,
> Since well I know
> To be my foe
> Her heart is firmly set.

> Since my intent,
> So truly meant,   10
> Cannot content
> Her mind as I do see,
> To tell you plain
> It were in vain
> For so small gain
> To lose my liberty.

> For if he thrive
> That will go strive
> A ship to drive
> Against the stream and wind,   20
> Undoubtedly
> Then thrive should I
> To love truly
> A cruel-hearted mind.

> But since that so
> The world doth go
> That every woe
> By yielding doth increase,
> As I have told
> I will be bold   30
> . . . .
> Thereby my pains to cease.

Praying you all
That after shall
By fortune fall
Into this foolish trade,
Have in your mind,
As I do find,
That oft by kind
All women's love do fade.   40

Wherefore apace,
Come take my place,
Some man that has
A lust to burn the feet;
For since that she
Refuseth me,
I must agree,
And study to forget.

47

Mistrustful minds be moved
To have me in suspect.
The truth it shall be proved,
Which time shall once detect.

Though falsehood go about
Of crime me to accuse,
At length I do not doubt
But truth shall me excuse.

Such sauce as they have served
To me without desert,   10
Even as they have deserved,
Thereof God send them part.

48

What should I say
Since faith is dead,
And truth away
From you is fled?
Should I be led
With doubleness?
Nay, nay, mistress.

I promised you
And you promised me,
To be as true   10
As I would be.
But since I see
Your double heart,
Farewell, my part.

Though for to take
It is not my mind,
But to forsake
One so unkind;
And as I find
So will I trust.   20
Farewell, unjust.

Can ye say nay
But that you said
That I alway
Should be obeyed?
And thus betrayed
Or that I wist,
Farewell, unkissed.

49

If chance assigned
Were to my mind
By very kind
Of destiny,
Yet would I crave
Naught else to have
But only life and liberty.

Then were I sure
I might endure
The displeasure   10
Of cruelty,
Where now I plain
Alas, in vain,
Lacking my life for liberty.

For without the one
The other is gone,
And there can none
It remedy:
If the one be past
The other doth waste,   20
And all for lack of liberty.

And so I drive,
As yet alive,
Although I strive
With misery;
Drawing my breath,
Looking for death
And loss of life for liberty.

But thou that still
Mayst at thy will   30
Turn all this ill
Adversity:
For the repair
Of my welfare
Grant me but life and liberty.

And if not so,
Then let all go
To wretched woe,
And let me die;
For the one or the other,   40
There is none other:
My death, or life with liberty.

50

Argument: Most wretched heart, most miserable,
Since the comfort is from thee fled,
Since all the truth is turned to fable,
Most wretched heart, why art thou not dead?

Reply: No, no, I live and must do still,
Whereof I thank God and no moe,
For I myself have at my will,
And he is wretched that weens him so.

Argument: But yet thou hast both had and lost
The hope so long that hath thee fed,   10
And all thy travail and thy cost:
Most wretched heart, why art thou not dead?

Reply: Some other hope must feed me new.
              If I have lost, I say 'What though?'
              Despair shall not through it ensue,
              For he is wretched that weens him so.

Argument: The sun, the moon doth frown on thee,
              Thou hast darkness in daylight's stead.
              As good in grave as so to be:
              Most wretched heart, why art thou not dead?   20

Reply: Some pleasant star may show me light,
              But though the heaven would work me woe,
              Who hath himself shall stand upright,
              And he is wretched that weens him so.

Argument: Hath he himself that is not sure?
              His trust is like as he hath sped;
              Against the stream thou mayst not dure:
              Most wretched heart, why art thou not dead?

Reply: The last is worst. Who fears not that,
              He hath himself whereso he go,   30
              And he that knoweth what is what
              Saith he is wretched that weens him so.

Argument: Seest thou not how they whet their teeth
              Which to touch thee sometime did dread?
              They find comfort for thy mischief:
              Most wretched heart, why art thou not dead?

Reply: What though that curse do fall by kind
              On him that hath the overthrow?
              All that cannot oppress my mind,
              For he is wretched that weens him so.   40

Argument: Yet can it not be then denied
           It is as certain as thy creed,
           Thy great unhap thou canst not hide:
           Unhappy then, why art thou not dead?

Reply: Unhappy, but no wretch therefore,
           For hap doth come again and go,
           For which I keep myself in store,
           Since unhap cannot kill me so.

51

Sufficèd not, madam, that you did tear
My woeful heart, but thus also to rent
The weeping paper that to you I sent,
Whereof each letter was written with a tear?

Could not my present pains, alas, suffice
Your greedy heart, and that my heart doth feel
Torments that prick more sharper than the steel,
But new and new must to my lot arise?

Use then my death. So shall your cruelty,
Spite of your spite, rid me from all my smart,   10
And I no more such torments of the heart
Feel as I do. This shalt thou gain thereby.

52

Spite hath no power to make me sad,
Nor scornfulness to make me plain.
It doth suffice that once I had,
And so to leave it is no pain.

Let them frown on that least doth gain;
Who did rejoice must needs be glad,
And though with words thou ween'st to reign,
It doth suffice that once I had.

Since that in checks thus overthwart
And coyly looks thou dost delight,   10
It does suffice that mine thou wert,
Though change hath put thy faith to flight.

Alas, it is a peevish spite
To yield thyself and then to part,
But since thou sett'st thy faith so light,
It doth suffice that mine thou wert.

And since thy love doth thus decline,
And in thy heart such hate doth grow,
It doth suffice that thou wert mine,
And with goodwill I quit it so.   20

Sometime my friend, farewell, my foe.
Since that thou change, I am not thine:
But for relief of all my woe
It doth suffice that thou wert mine.

Praying you all that hears this song
To judge no wight, nor none to blame:
It doth suffice she doth me wrong,
And that herself doth know the same.

And though she change, it is no shame:
Their kind it is, and hath been long.   30
Yet I protest she hath no name:
It doth suffice she doth me wrong.

53
Ye know my heart, my lady dear,
That since the time I was your thrall
I have been yours both whole and clear,
Though my reward hath been but small:
So am I yet and more than all.
And ye know well how I have served,
As if ye prove it shall appear
    How well, how long,
    How faithfully,
    And suffered wrong   10
    How patiently.
Then since that I have never swerved,
Let not my pains be undeserved.

Ye know also, though ye say nay,
That you alone are my desire,
And you alone it is that may
Assuage my fervent flaming fire.
Succour me then, I you require.
Ye know it were a just request,
Since ye do cause my heat, I say,   20
    If that I burn
    That ye will warm,
    And not turn
    All to my harm,
Sending such flame from frozen breast
Against all right for my unrest.

And I know well how frowardly
Ye have mista'en my true intent,
And hitherto how wrongfully
I have found cause for to repent.   30
But death shall rid me readily
If your hard heart do not relent;
And I know well all this ye know
    That I and mine
    And all I have
    Ye may assign
    To spill or save.
Why are ye then so cruel foe
Unto your own that loves you so.

54

Process of time worketh such wonder
That water, which is of kind so soft,
Doth pierce the marble stone asunder
By little drops falling from aloft.

And yet a heart that seems so tender
Receiveth no drop of the stilling tears,
That alway still cause me to render
The vain plaint that sounds not in her ears.

So cruel, alas, is naught alive,
So fierce, so froward, so out of frame,   10
But some way, some time may so contrive
By means the wild to temper and tame.

And I that always have sought and seek
Each place, each time, for some lucky day,
This fierce tiger, less I find her meek,
And more denied the longer I pray.

The lion in his raging furor
Forbears that sueth meakness, for his boot;
And thou, alas, in extreme dolour
The heart so low thou treads under foot.   20

Each fierce thing, lo, how thou dost exceed
And hides it under so humble a face.
And yet the humble to help at need
Naught helpeth time, humbleness, nor place.

55
Such hap as I am happèd in
Had never man of truth, I ween.
At me Fortune list to begin
To show that never hath been seen,
A new kind of unhappiness.
Nor I cannot the thing I mean
        Myself express.

Myself express my deadly pain,
That can I well if that might serve;
But why I have not help again,   10
That know I not unless I sterve
For hunger still amidst my food,
So granted is that I deserve
        To do me good.

To do me good what may prevail?
For I deserve and not desire,
And still of cold I me bewail,
And rakèd am in burning fire.
For though I have, such is my lot,
In hand to help that I require,   20
        It helpeth not.

It helpeth not but to increase
That that by proof can be no more:
That is the heat that cannot cease,
And that I have, to crave so sore.
What wonder is this greedy lust
To ask and have, and yet therefore
    Refrain I must.

Refrain I must. What is the cause?
Sure, as they say, 'So hawks be taught.'   30
But in my case layeth no such cause,
For with such craft I am not caught.
Wherefore I say, and good cause why,
With hapless hand no man hath raught
    Such hap as I.

56
Take heed betime lest ye be spied.
Your loving eyes ye cannot hide.
At last the truth will sure be tried.
    Therefore take heed!

For some there be of crafty kind,
Though you show no part of your mind,
Surely their eyes ye cannot blind.
    Therefore take heed!

For in like case theirselves hath been,
And thought right sure none had them seen;   10
But it was not as they did ween.
    Therefore take heed!

Although they be of diverse schools
And well can use all crafty tools,
At length they prove themselves but fools.
        Therefore take heed!

If they might take you in that trap,
They would soon leave it in your lap.
To love unspied is but a hap:
        Therefore take heed!   20

57
Forget not yet the tried intent
Of such a truth as I have meant,
My great travail so gladly spent,
        Forget not yet.

Forget not yet when first began
The weary life ye know since when,
The suit, the service none tell can,
        Forget not yet.

Forget not yet the great assays,
The cruel wrong, the scornful ways,   10
The painful patience in denays,
        Forget not yet.

Forget not yet, forget not this,
How long ago hath been and is
The mind that never meant amiss,
        Forget not yet.

Forget not then thine own approved,
The which so long hath thee so loved,
Whose steadfast faith yet never moved,
        Forget not this.

58

Your looks so often cast,
Your eyes so friendly rolled,
Your sight fixèd so fast,
Always one to behold;
Though hide it fain ye would,
It plainly doth declare
Who hath your heart in hold
And where good will ye bear.

Fain would ye find a cloak
Your burning fire to hide,   10
Yet both the flame and smoke
Breaks out on every side.
Ye cannot love so guide
That it no issue win;
Abroad needs must it glide
That burns so hot within.

For cause yourself do wink,
Ye judge all other blind,
And secret it you think,
Which every man doth find.   20
In waste oft spend ye wind,
Yourself in love to quit,
For agues of that kind
Will show who hath the fit.

Your sighs you fet from far,
And all to wry your woe.
Yet are you ne'er the nar:
Men are not blinded so.
Deeply oft swear ye no,
But all those oaths are vain,   30
So well your eye doth show
Who puts your heart to pain.

71

Think not therefore to hide
That still itself betrays,
Nor seek means to provide
To dark the sunny days.
Forget those wonted ways,
Leave off such frowning cheer.
There will be found no stays
To stop a thing so clear.   40

59

Ah, my heart, ah, what aileth thee
To set so light my liberty,
Making me bound when I was free,
Ah, my heart, ah, what aileth thee?

When thou were rid from all distress,
Void of all pain and pensiveness,
To choose again a new mistress,
Ah, my heart, ah, what aileth thee?

When thou were well, thou could not hold;
To turn again, that were too bold.   10
Thus to renew my sorrows old,
Ah, my heart, ah, what aileth thee?

Thou know'st full well that but of late
I was turned out of Love's gate:
And now to guide me to this mate,
Ah, my heart, ah, what aileth thee?

I hoped full well all had been done,
But now my hope is ta'en and won.
To my torment to yield so soon,
Ah, my heart, ah, what aileth thee?   20

60

To make an end of all this strife,
No longer time for to sustain,
But now with death to change the life
Of him that lives always in pain;
Despair such power hath in his hand
That helpeth most, I know certain,
     May not withstand.

May not withstand that is elect
By Fortune's most extremity,
But all in worth to be except   10
Withouten law or liberty;
What vaileth then unto my thought?
If right can have no remedy,
     There vaileth naught.

There vaileth naught, but all is vain.
The fault thereof may none amend,
But only death, for to constrain
This spiteful hap to have an end.
So great disdain doth me provoke,
That dread of death cannot defend   20
     This deadly stroke.

This deadly stroke, whereby shall cease
The harboured sighs within my heart,
And for the gift of this release
My hand in haste shall play his part
To do this cure against his kind,
For change of life from long desert
     To place assigned.

To place assigned for evermore.
Now by constraint I do agree
To loose the bond of my restore,
Wherein is bound my liberty.
Death and despair doth undertake
From all mishap now hardily
    This end to make.

30

61

    If in the world there be more woe
        Than I have in my heart,
    Whereso it is, it doth come fro,
    And in my breast there doth it grow,
        For to increase my smart.
Alas, I am receipt of every care,
And of my life each sorrow claims his part.
        Who list to live in quietness
        By me let him beware,
        For I by high disdain
        Am mad without redress,
    And unkindness, alas, hath slain
    My poor true heart all comfortless.

10

62

My love is like unto th'eternal fire,
And I as those which therein do remain,
Whose grievous pains is but their great desire
To see the sight which they may not attain.
So in hell's heat myself I feel to be,
That am restrained by great extremity,
The sight of her which is so dear to me.
O puissant love and power of great avail,
By whom hell may be felt or death assail.

74

63

Disdain me not without desert,
Nor leave me not so suddenly,
Since well ye wot that in my heart
I mean it not but honestly,
    Refuse me not.

Refuse me not without cause why,
Nor think me not to be unjust,
Since that by lot of fantasy
The careful knot needs knit I must,
    Mistrust me not.   10

Mistrust me not, though some there be
That fain would spot my steadfastness;
Believe them not since well ye see
The proof is not as they express:
    Forsake me not.

Forsake me not till I deserve,
Nor hate me not till I offend,
Destroy me not till that I swerve:
Since ye well wot what I intend
    Disdain me not.   20

Disdain me not that am your own,
Refuse me not that am so true,
Mistrust me not till all be known,
Forsake me not now for no new:
    Disdain me not.

Satires

64

Mine own John Poyntz, since ye delight to know
    The cause why that homeward I me draw,
    And flee the press of courts whereso they go
Rather than to live thrall under the awe
    Of lordly looks, wrapped within my cloak,
    To will and lust learning to set a law:
It is not because I scorn or mock
    The power of them to whom Fortune hath lent
    Charge over us, of right, to strike the stroke;
But true it is that I have always meant   10
    Less to esteem them than the common sort,
    Of outward things that judge in their intent
Without regard what doth inward resort.
    I grant sometime that of glory the fire
    Doth touch my heart: me list not to report
Blame by honour and honour to desire,
    But how may I this honour now attain
    That cannot dye the colour black a liar?
My Poyntz, I cannot frame my tune to feign,
    To cloak the truth for praise, without desert   20
    Of them that list all vice for to retain.
I cannot honour them that sets their part
    With Venus and Bacchus all their life long,
    Nor hold my peace of them although I smart.
I cannot crouch nor kneel to do so great a wrong
    To worship them like God on earth alone
    That are as wolves these silly lambs among.
I cannot with my words complain and moan
    And suffer naught, nor smart without complaint,
    Nor turn the word that from my mouth is gone.   30
I cannot speak and look like a saint,
    Use wiles for wit and make deceit a pleasure,

And call craft counsel, for profit still to paint.
I cannot wrest the law to fill the coffer,
    With innocent blood to feed myself fat,
    And do most hurt where most help I offer.
I am not he that can allow the state
    Of high Caesar and damn Cato to die,
    That with his death did 'scape out of the gate
From Caesar's hands, if Livy do not lie,   40
    And would not live where liberty was lost,
    So did his heart the common wealth apply.
I am not he such eloquence to boast
    To make the crow singing as the swan,
    Nor call the lion of coward beasts the most
That cannot take a mouse as the cat can;
    And he that dieth for hunger of the gold,
    Call him Alexander, and say that Pan
Passeth Apollo in music many fold,
    Praise Sir Thopas for a noble tale   50
    And scorn the story that the knight told;
Praise him for counsel that is drunk of ale,
    Grin when he laugheth that beareth all the sway,
    Frown when he frowneth and groan when he is pale,
On other's lust to hang both night and day.
    None of these points would ever frame in me.
    My wit is naught, I cannot learn the way.
And much the less of things that greater be,
    That asken help of colours of device
    To join the mean with each extremity: 60
With nearest virtue to cloak alway the vice,
    And as to purpose likewise it shall fall
    To press the virtue that it may not rise,
As drunkenness good fellowship to call,
    The friendly foe with his double face
    Say he is gentle and courteous therewithal,
And say that Favel hath a goodly grace
    In eloquence, and cruelty to name

Zeal of justice and change in time and place;
And he that suffereth offence without blame,   70
    Call him pitiful, and him true and plain
    That raileth reckless to every man's shame;
Say he is rude that cannot lie and feign,
    The lecher a lover, and tyranny
    To be the right of a prince's reign.
I cannot I; no, no, it will not be!
    This is the cause that I could never yet
    Hang on their sleeves that weigh, as thou mayst see,
A chip of chance more than a pound of wit.
    This maketh me at home to hunt and to hawk,   80
    And in foul weather at my book to sit;
In frost and snow then with my bow to stalk.
    No man doth mark whereso I ride or go;
    In lusty leas at liberty I walk.
And of these news I feel nor weal nor woe,
    Save that a clog doth hang yet at my heel.
    No force for that, for it is ordered so
That I may leap both hedge and dike full well.
    I am not now in France to judge the wine,
    With savoury sauce the delicates to feel;   90
Nor yet in Spain, where one must him incline,
    Rather than to be, outwardly to seem.
    I meddle not with wits that be so fine,
Nor Flanders cheer letteth not my sight to deem
    Of black and white, nor taketh my wit away
    With beastliness, they beasts do so esteem.
Nor I am not where Christ is given in prey
    For money, poison, and treason, at Rome –
    A common practice used night and day.
But here I am in Kent and Christendom,   100
    Among the Muses where I read and rhyme,
    Where if thou list, my Poyntz, for to come,
Thou shalt be judge how I do spend my time.

65

'A spending hand that alway poureth out
    Had need to have a bringer-in as fast';
    And 'On the stone that still doth turn about
There groweth no moss.' These proverbs yet do last.
    Reason hath set them in so sure a place
    That length of years their force can never waste.
When I remember this and eke the case
    Wherein thou stands, I thought forthwith to write,
    Bryan, to thee, who knows how great a grace
In writing is to counsel man the right.   10
    To thee, therefore, that trots still up and down
    And never rests, but running day and night
From realm to realm, from city, street, and town,
    Why dost thou wear thy body to the bones
    And mightst at home sleep in thy bed of down,
And drink good ale so nappy for the nonce,
    Feed thyself fat and heap up pound by pound?
    Likest thou not this? No, why? 'For swine so groins
In sty and chaw the turds moulded on the ground,
    And drivel on pearls, the head still in the manger,   20
    Then of the harp the ass do hear the sound.
So sacks of dirt be filled up in the cloister
    That serves for less than do these fatted swine.
    Though I seem lean and dry without moisture,
Yet will I serve my prince, my lord and thine,
    And let them live to feed the paunch that list,
    So I may feed to live, both me and mine.'
By God, well said. But what and if thou wist
    How to bring in as fast as thou dost spend?
    'That would I learn.' And it shall not be missed   30
To tell thee how. Now hark what I intend.
    Thou knowest well first whoso can seek to please
    Shall purchase friends where truth shall but offend.
Flee therefore truth: it is both wealth and ease.
    For though that truth of every man hath praise,

Full near that wind go'th truth in great misease.
Use virtue as it goeth nowadays,
    In word alone to make thy language sweet,
    And of the deed yet do not as thou says,
Else be thou sure thou shalt be far unmeet   40
    To get thy bread, each thing is now so scant.
    Seek still thy profit upon thy bare feet.
Lend in no wise, for fear that thou do want,
    Unless it be as to a dog a cheese,
    By which return be sure to win a cant
Or half at least: it is not good to leese.
    Learn at Kitson, that in a long white coat
    From under the stall without lands or fees
Hath leapt into the shop, who knoweth by rote
    This rule that I have told thee herebefore.   50
    Sometime also rich age beginneth to dote;
See thou when there thy gain may be the more.
    Stay him by the arm whereso he walk or go,
    Be near alway and, if he cough too sore,
When he hath spit, tread out and please him so.
    A diligent knave that picks his master's purse
    May please him so that he, withouten moe,
Executor is, and what is he the worse?
    But if so chance you get naught of the man,
    The widow may for all thy charge deburse.   60
A rivelled skin, a stinking breath, what then?
    A toothless mouth shall do thy lips no harm.
    The gold is good, and though she curse or ban,
Yet where thee list thou mayst lie good and warm.
    Let the old mule bite upon the bridle
    Whilst there do lie a sweeter in thine arm.
In this also see you be not idle:
    Thy niece, thy cousin, thy sister, or thy daughter,
    If she be fair, if handsome be her middle,
If thy better hath her love besought her,   . 70
    Advance his cause and he shall help thy need.

It is but love, turn it to a laughter.
But ware, I say, so gold thee help and speed,
    That in this case thou be not so unwise
    As Pandar was in such a like deed,
For he, the fool of conscience, was so nice
    That he no gain would have for all his pain.
    Be next thyself, for friendship bears no prize.
Laugh'st thou at me? Why? Do I speak in vain?
    'No, not at thee, but at thy thrifty jest.   80
    Wouldst thou I should, for any loss or gain,
Change that for gold that I have ta'en for best,
    Next godly things, to have an honest name?
    Should I leave that? Then take me for a beast.'
Nay then, farewell, and if you care for shame,
    Content thee then with honest poverty,
    With free tongue, what thee mislikes, to blame,
And, for thy truth, sometime adversity,
    And therewithal this thing I shall thee give:
    In this world now, little prosperity,   90
And coin to keep, as water in a sieve.

Paraphrase of Penitential Psalms

66 *Psalm No. 102, 'Hear my prayer, O Lord'*
Lord, hear my prayer and let my cry pass
    Unto thee, Lord, without impediment.
    Do not from me turn thy merciful face,
Unto myself leaving my government.
    In time of trouble and adversity
    Incline to me thine ear and thine intent;
And when I call, help my necessity;
    Readily grant th'effect of my desire.
    These bold demands do please thy majesty,
And eke my case such haste doth well require.　　　　　　　10
    For like as smoke my days been passed away,
    My bones dried up as furnace with the fire.
My heart, my mind is withered up like hay
    Because I have forgot to take my bread,
    My bread of life, the word of truth, I say.
And for my plaintful sighs and my dread,
    My bones, my strength, my very force of mind
    Cleaved to the flesh and from thy sprite were fled,
As desperate thy mercy for to find.
    So made I me the solaine pelican　　　　　　　20
    And like the owl that flyeth by proper kind
Light of the day and hath herself beta'en
    To ruin life out of all company.
    With waker care that with this woe began,
Like the sparrow was I solitary,
    That sits alone under the house's eaves.
    This while my foes conspired continually
And did provoke the harm of my disease.
    Wherefore like ashes my bread did me savour;
    Of thy just word the taste might not me please.　　　　　30
Wherefore my drink I tempered with liquor
    Of weeping tears that from mine eyes do rain,

Because I know the wrath of thy furor,
Provoked by right, had of my pride disdain
    For thou didst lift me up to throw me down,
    To teach me how to know myself again;
Whereby I know that helpless I should drown.
    My days like shadow decline and I do dry,
    And thee forever eternity doth crown;
World without end doth last thy memory.   40
    For this frailty that yoketh all mankind,
    Thou shalt awake and rue this misery,
Rue on Zion, Zion that, as I find,
    Is the people that live under thy law;
    For now is time, the time at hand assigned,
The time so long that doth thy servants draw
    In great desire to see that pleasant day,
    Day of redeeming Zion from sin's awe.
For they have ruth to see in such decay,
    In dust and stones, this wretched Zion lower.   50
    Then the gentiles shall dread thy name alway;
All earthly kings thy glory shall honour,
    Then when thy grace this Zion thus redeemeth,
    When thus thou hast declared thy mighty power.
The Lord his servants' wishes so esteemeth
    That he him turn'th unto the poors' request.
    To our descent this to be written seemeth,
Of all comforts, as consolation best;
    And they that then shall be regenerate
    Shall praise the Lord therefore, both most and least.   60
For he hath looked from the height of his estate;
    The Lord from heaven in earth hath looked on us,
    To hear the moan of them that are algate
In foul bondage, to loose and to discuss
    The sons of death out from their deadly bond,
    To give thereby occasion gracious
In this Zion his holy name to stand
    And in Jerusalem his lauds, lasting ay,

When in one church the people of the land
And realms been gathered to serve, to laud, to pray   70
  The Lord above so just and merciful.
  But to this sembly running in the way
My strength faileth to reach it at the full.
  He hath abridged my days; they may not dure
  To see that term, that term so wonderful,
Although I have with hearty will and cure
  Prayed to the Lord: 'Take me not, Lord, away
  In mids of my years, though thine ever sure
Remain eterne, whom time cannot decay.
  Thou wrought'st the earth; thy hands th'heavens did make;
  They shall perish and thou shalt last alway.   [80
And all things age shall wear and overtake
  Like cloth, and thou shalt change them like apparel,
  Turn and translate, and they in worth it take.
But thou thyself the self remainest well
  That thou wast erst, and shalt thy years extend.
  Then since to this there may nothing rebel,
The greatest comfort that I can pretend
  Is that the children of thy servants dear,
  That in thy word are got, shall without end   90
Before thy face be stablished all in fere.'

67 *Psalm No. 130, 'Out of the deep have I called'*
From depth of sin and from a deep despair,
    From depth of death, from depth of heart's sorrow,
    From this deep cave of darkness' deep repair,
Thee have I called, O Lord, to be my borrow.
    Thou in my voice, O Lord, perceive and hear
    My heart, my hope, my plaint, my overthrow,
My will to rise, and let by grant appear
    That to my voice, thine ears do well intend.
    No place so far that to thee is not near;
No depth so deep that thou ne mayst extend   10
    Thine ear thereto. Hear then my woeful plaint.
    For Lord, if thou do observe what men offend
And put thy native mercy in restraint,
    If just exaction demand recompense,
    Who may endure, O Lord? Who shall not faint
At such account? Dread and not reverence
    Should so reign large. But thou seeks rather love,
    For in thy hand is mercy's residence,
By hope whereof thou dost our hearts move.
    I in thee, Lord, have set my confidence;   20
    My soul such trust doth evermore approve.
Thy holy word of eterne excellence,
    Thy mercy's promise that is alway just,
    Have been my stay, my pillar, and pretence.
My soul in God hath more desirous trust
    Than hath the watchman looking for the day,
    By the relief to quench of sleep the thrust.
Let Israel trust unto the Lord alway
    For grace and favour are his property.
    Plenteous ransom shall come with him, I say,   30
And shall redeem all our iniquity.

Notes

1: W uses the hind to symbolize a love chase, the futility of which causes him to withdraw. The sonnet is generally considered to refer to W's relationship with Anne Boleyn. 1, *list:* chooses; 3, *vain travail:* useless effort; 6, *deer:* pun on dear; 11, *diamonds:* M&T point out that in Petrarch diamonds are 'symbols of chastity'; 13: do not touch me, for I am the king's.

2: 6, *scape:* escape; *no wise:* in no way; 7, *device:* wish, inclination; 9, *eyen:* eyes; *plain:* complain.

3: 1, *charged with forgetfulness:* 'oppressed by love so as to forget all else' (Tillyard); 2, *thorough:* through; 3, *eke:* also; *mine enemy:* love; 5-6: ready to think that death is of little consequence; 12, *stars:* the lady's eyes.

4: An obscure poem. Perhaps he is dreaming about fulfilled love, only to awaken to find the lady not there; her image has disappeared 'into this tossing mew'. Thus only his spirit (the dream state) 'had his desire'. But that state, although wished, could not remain or become reality. Thus the dream mocks him. 1, *according:* appropriate; 3, *rue:* regret; 5, *by good respect:* after proper consideration; 6, *mew:* cage, in which hawks were kept, used figuratively, perhaps for the poet's bed or, more likely, his state of mind before waking; 7, *sprite:* his spirit in the dream state; 9: his body asleep, his spirit 'had his desire'; 11-12: why didn't it stay in the dream state instead of returning to consciousness?

5: 2, *to plain:* to complain; 3, *distain:* discolour, his blushing and going pale; 8, *Brunet:* Anne Boleyn. W altered the line, which originally read, 'Her that did set our country in a roar'; 9, *Phyllis:* Probably W's later mistress, Elizabeth Darrell; 14, *scant:* scarcely.

6: Considered to be a lament for his patron, Thomas Cromwell, executed on 28 July 1540. If so, the self-hate can only be explained by his failed diplomacy in Spain, during which he had to serve with Cromwell's enemy, the Duke of Norfolk. 5, *unhap:* misfortune; *hap:* luck, chance; 11, *plaint:* complaint, grief; 12, *smart:* pain, suffering.

7: This sonnet might refer to W's imprisonment in May 1534 and 1536. Chaucer often refers to May as an unfortunate time, and lines 3-4 would seem to derive from the last two lines of stanza 16, Book II of *Troilus and Criseyde*. 2, *lust:* pleasure; 3, *sluggardy:* laziness; 5, *in mischance:* in bad luck or misfortune; 6, *haps:* happenings; 7, *me betide:* happened to me; 9, *Sephame:* Edward Sephame, an astrologer, who presumably had cast W's horoscope.

8: 1-2: he thought it cruel for her to scorn his love, yet retain his service; 4, *which:* who; 5, *care:* this pain or sorrow; 6, *Displease thee not:* Don't be displeased that my days of doting on you are over.

9: Probably written in prison in 1541, describing his physical and mental state. See also 15 and 17. 7-8, Ironically, although physically wasted to deathly colour he is still aware of the sweetness (pleasure) in pain; 9, *list:* chooses; 10, *can force:* can matter; 12, *no force:* no matter; 15, *But you:* his friend, Sir Francis Bryan; 18, *there is no great desert:* I have done nothing to deserve this punishment; 20: Saw the shadow of misfortune that you continue to know about; 25, *she:* his fever; *list assign:* wishes to assign, is responsible for his burning heat.

10: 2, *And after the old proverb:* Chaucer – 'He hasteth wel that wisely kan abyde'; 5, *tarry the tide:* abide my time; 6, *ye:* the lady; 7, *wot:* know; 10, *sayeth:* as they say; 13, *plain:* to speak plainly; 14, *shall not obtain:* refuse me my desire.

11: 1, *hap:* good luck; 3: Whether he gives up his hope of good luck, or continues to hope, it is equally painful; 9, *this:* this relationship, or condition; 10, *rightwisely:* righteously; 11, *Leave:* lives; *again:* against.

12: Compare Skelton's *Philip Sparrow* (26-29 and 35-43); 2, *plaint:* complaint; *remembered her my woe:* reminded her of my woe.

13: 1: death; 4: Cleanly to get rid of the fever caused by his love; 8: Obscure, but apparently means that the fever of his love is made worse by the proposed remedy of ridding his body of it?

14: Refers to W leaving Spain in June 1539 and returning to London; 2: the famously gold sands of the river Tagus; 5, *the town which Brutus sought:* London.

15: Probably written during W's imprisonment in 1541; 6: W is assaulted by malice – the motive of Bonner's false charges against him, and only his own righteousness can save him; 7, *Bryan:* the fellow courtier, poet and diplomat, Sir Francis Bryan; 7-8: proverb which W used in his defence, saying that his accusers thought it was enough just to accuse him. 'For tho he hele the wounde yet the scharre shall remayne' (Muir).

16: E.K. Chambers and others suggest this is a portrait of Elizabeth Darrell, and the last line seems to confirm it, although Fx favours Howard's sister, Mary Duchess of Richmond.

17: Probably written during W's imprisonment in 1541, but Southall thinks 1534 and that Lux is Anne Boleyn, 'who was represented in her coronation pageants as a white falcon'. The first line, however, does refer to 'your fellows all'. 1, *Lux:* name of a falcon; 1-2: reference to

Cromwell – to whom liberty would have been as pleasant as to a falcon – not forsaking W, but if Southall is right it refers to freedom from Anne's affections; 7-8: only his birds remain his true friends.

18: Popular in W's time. In 1565 John Hall converted it to a religious parody, beginning, 'My lute awake! and praise the Lord'. 7-8: As soon as lead is able to engrave on marble – namely, never – his song may pierce her heart; 17, *thorough:* through; 19: Don't think Cupid will let you off lightly. He will wreak vengeance (l.21); 24, *unquit:* without punishment, unrequited; *plain:* complaint; 27, *winter nights:* during the winter nights; 28, *plaining:* complaining; 30, *list:* pleases.

19: Another victim of Hall's moralizing – 'Blame not my lute though it do sound/The rebuke of your wicked sin'. 2, *as liketh me:* as pleases me; 6, *speaks:* speak; 19, *indite:* compose, write; 26, *desert:* deserving.

20: 4, *to let:* to go free; 5-8: Why should he hide the pain he feels when his music can ease it?; 11 and 59, *all other suit:* all other entreaty; 24, *wot:* know; 39, *beseek:* beseech.

21: 1, *in eternum:* Forever, unto eternity; *determed:* determined; 1-3: he once determined to love some woman forever; determined, affirmed and confirmed probably had the last syllable accented; 9, *press:* he determined to pursue this course; 14, *troth had taken place:* his faithfulness, commitment to her had been accepted by her forever; 17-20: It was not long before he found that this was not so; 21-24: He cast out from his heart forever his original concept of fidelity and has replaced it with another idea, another thought, perhaps another love.

22: Popular song, another version of which is sung by Feste in *Twelfth Night*. 2, *jolly:* gentle; 3, *leman:* lover, in this case the lady; 5, *perdie:* an oath, By God, verily; 8, *yet:* still; 15-16: a proverb; 27-28: Seek your satisfaction in the wives of other men, thus avoiding the disappointment of being deserted by a woman you trusted.

23: 8, *Departed right:* 'separated in just proportion one from another' (Nott); 10, *Goodly begone:* 'beautifully adorned' or 'exquisitely fashioned in itself' (Tillyard); 18, *repair:* adorn; 21, *demesne:* possession; 23, *to rue:* to take pity; 24, *reach me:* extend to me; 27, *strain:* 'increase the torment so as to reduce a person to the last extremity' (Nott).

24: 1, *Perdie:* By God, verily, truly; 8, *straiter:* tighter; 24, *lust:* pleasure; 30, *plaint:* complaint, grief; 33, *fro:* from; 35-36: Is the allegation, the rumour, invented to cause him more pain? 37-40: Having falsely made the charge, she should, with the same vigour, repress it; 45-46: See Genesis, Chapter 29 for story of how, on Jacob's marriage, Laban deceived him and substituted his elder daughter, Leah, for the younger Rachel.

25: 3, *bourds:* jests; 4, *show it so:* show that you are willing; 5, *beck:* a nod, gesture; 9, *fain:* pleased; 12: I'll be my own master again, not your servant.

26: Addressed either to a woman (D uses 'she' throughout) or to former friends (E uses 'they') now perhaps political enemies. 3, *God wot:* God knows; 13, *withouten blame:* when he is blameless; 14, *naught:* not; 19: Patience in all the harm done to him.

27: D has 'meaneth' in lines 1 and 20 only. I have used 'means' to preserve the octosyllabic line. 13, *A mornings:* In the mornings; 14, *guise:* usual mode of behaviour; 15, *devise:* try to conjecture; 30-31: Nothing has been achieved in all this time except the frustration of his love, that he fears most.

28: 5, *in danger:* in my power; 10: In a pleasing and fashionable thin gown; 16, *thorough:* through; 18, *of her goodness:* because of her goodness; 19: *newfangleness:* A Chaucerian word meaning fickleness, inconstancy; 20, *kindly:* Trisyllabic, kindely? Used ironically – in a kind manner and also in accordance with the law of kind or nature, in this case, the faithlessness of women.

29: 2, *will:* self-will; 4, *Indian sea;* the furthest distance; 5, *Thule:* the most distant point, Greek name 'for a land six days' sail north of Britain' (*OED*); 8-12: God who made the stars made also man for noble purposes; 18, *precious:* probably a trisyllable; 19 *Ycharged:* probably Ychargèd, burdened; *covetise:* greed; 20-21: Obscure, but suggest that covetous concern for wealth cannot prevent life being wretched, nor profit one in death. 21, *nor:* MS has ne.

30: Rebholz suggests that 'dear heart' (l.5) could refer not only to 'the speaker's lady' but also 'to the speaker's own heart', giving double meanings throughout. 7, *smart:* pain; 16, *wonderly:* wondrously; 24: Except that he continues to have what he has now – namely, on the first meaning, his lady's love; 27, *suffrance:* suffering; *redress:* reparation; 28, *hire:* reward.

31: 3, *weal:* well-being; 9, *bootless:* useless; 12, *I drive:* I hasten, go; 16, *recure:* cure; 18, *ban:* curse.

32: 5, *rue:* have pity; 6, *your thrall:* your slave, your servant.

33: 4, *grame:* sorrow; 9, *among:* all the time.

34: 1, *will needs:* demand; 2: accept my singing for what it's worth; 5, *Bootless for boot:* without receiving any reward or advantage; 9: to go without food and lie awake in bed; 10-12: The temper of his song is such that he cries of the wrong done to him so much that paradoxically he lacks tears to bewail the wrong. 18, *plain:* complain; 27 *pleasant game* is meant ironically.

35: 5, 10, 15, 20, 25, 30, *Alas the while!:* Alas the time, as an expression of grief. 19, *remove:* change her affection.

36: 13, *diverse mind:* variety of feeling; 17, *To spy it:* to see the truth (of a person); 18, *die:* dice; 24, *fall highest:* fall from the highest place; 27, *Whoso list:* whoever chooses; 28, *preve:* prove.

37: Nott and M&T suggest the poem is addressed to Mary Souche, one of Jane Seymour's maids of honour. 7, *moe:* more; 9, *smart:* pain; 15, *Overthwart:* perverse, unfavourable; 24, *to lour:* to look darkly, scowl; 27, 29, 31, *such:* punning on Mary Souche?

38: 1 and 22, *love's:* probably disyllabic; 2, *torment:* tormented; 14, *proveth:* perhaps prov'th; 31, *lime;* bird-lime, a sticky substance used to catch birds; 34, *scaped:* escaped.

39: 7, *gan:* began; 12: Had been dumb and not moved at all; 13, *aught:* anything; 17-18: Then he could not walk; 21, *relent:* yield; 22, *spill:* kill, ruin.

40: 2, *sue:* pursue; 7, *list:* chooses; *lour:* to be overcast or to scowl; 23, *mischief:* distress, sorrow; 33, *rede:* advice, there is no useful advice for a person in despair; 34: speech is no use to someone without an ear; 35: although alive, he might as well be dead.

41: The jerky rhythm suggests apprehension and uncertainty, and more, I think, about some political situation (see lines 8/9) than about love; 5, *windy words:* vain, empty words; *quaint:* cunning; 7, 14, 21: He doesn't take up a permanent position (or completely trust some other person) lest he should fall. 10, *hase:* (as in E) probably meaning hazard. 11: Refers back to maze, in which he can wander but not get out of. He is thus 'imprisoned in liberties', unable to decide; 13, *naught:* nothing; 15: Although he has had assurances, he doubts them. In fact, he cannot be sure, either of the assurances or of his doubt. W is being deliberately ambiguous, and different punctuation could produce different meanings; 17 *in ure:* in use; 18, *trusty:* trustworthy.

42: 3, *lust:* pleasure; 5: More haste less speed; 8-9: Why was I certain in my opinion of the other person (or situation) without some displeasure? 11, *revolted:* turned; 12, *wonderly:* wondrously; 20: Since my faithfulness was the cause of my boldness; 24, *among:* all the time; 25, *hap:* good fortune; 26, *happed:* happened; 27, *Assurance:* his apparent certainty; 29, *note:* his manner, the tune he sings; 31, *burden:* the weight of sorrow; 33: Because the tune has changed, what had once seemed the steadfastness of the relationship now gives no pleasure.

91

43: In W's hand with many revisions and alterations. Fx thinks it was written in Spain, but Tillyard suggests it was written after W's return. 2, *plague:* W originally wrote 'poison'; 6: The body that has no sleep wears itself away; 9-10: The wound, though cured, leaves its scar, and the flesh never returns to its normal condition; 11: Take pleasure in his goodly turn (his trick), meant ironically; 15, *fell:* fierce, an odd repetition; *recure:* cure, remedy; 17-20: If not by me, may you never be loved again, especially by whoever else you now love, and may you, justly, suffer the disdain of your love, because of your cruelty to me. 20, *threat:* threaten, menace.

44: 1, *mischief:* distress, sorrow; 26, *pervert:* perverted; 31, *spill:* destroy; 38, *lust:* desire.

45: 4, *plain:* complain; 12, *ye list:* you choose.

46: 2, *refuse:* refusal; 29, *told:* said; 30: After this line there appears to be a line missing; 38, *by kind:* by its nature.

47: 2, *suspect:* suspicion; 4, *once:* one day.

48: 14, *part:* his part of the relationship; 15-21: It is not his intention to continue the relationship; he has found her unjust, and so, 'farewell'; 18, Nott's suggestion for missing line; 22-23: Can you deny that you said; 27, *wist:* knew.

49: This could be a poem about the life and liberty he would experience if he could escape the cruelty of loving a certain woman, but to me it makes greater sense for the poem to be about his desire to be freed from restrictions imposed upon his life, perhaps by imprisonment, especially suggested by the second stanza. 20-21: There's no life (it wastes away) without liberty; 22, *drive:* suffer; 27-28: Death would bring liberty.

50: Perhaps written in Spain, or later, and concerned with the enmity of Bonner. 6, *no moe:* no more; 7: He is in control of himself; 8, 16, 24, 32, 40: He is wretched who believes, or thinks, himself so – adapted from Chaucer's *The Playnte to Fortune*; 13, *new:* anew; 26: He has no trust in himself, 'future expectations are no brighter than past experience' (Tillyard); 27, *dure:* endure; 29, *The last:* death; 35, *mischief:* distress; 43: *unhap:* misfortune; 46, *hap:* luck.

51: 2, *to rent:* to tear; 12: His death would be her gain. It has been suggested that a final couplet is missing, but the poem is complete as it is.

52: 3, *that once I had:* once I had both her and her love; 5-6: Those who have enjoyed least favours, let them frown, but those who enjoyed their love must be glad; 7, *ween'st:* hope. I have used an apostrophe to preserve the octosyllabic line. 9-10: Since in rebuke or censure, she delights in cross and coy looks; 26, *wight:* human being; 31: He is not prepared to name her.

53: 2, *thrall:* slave; 22, *warm:* grow warm; 27, *frowardly:* perversely, unreasonably; 29-30: He has had wrongly to repent for intentions perversely interpreted by the lady; 34: Southall assumes that 'this is an appeal to Anne Boleyn whose own motto was "Me and Mine".' 36, *assign:* decide, determine; 37, *spill:* kill – the phrase was conventional in courtly love.

54: 6, *stilling:* distilling; 10, *froward:* perverse; 9-12: Nothing is so cruel and perverse that some way cannot be found to tame it. 13-16: He likens the lady to a fierce tiger, and has sought the lucky day when he might tame her, but the more he pleads the more he is denied. 18: Pursues meekness as a reward (boot). 23-24: Neither time, humbleness nor place can make the proud (her) help the humble (him).

55: 1-7: Seemingly, the lady he loves, and who loves him, will not sexually satisfy him. Such an unlucky situation – designed by Fortune – is a new kind of unhappiness, and he doesn't know how to explain it himself. 2, *ween:* think; 10-14: He cannot understand why he is starved of love for his own good; 11, *sterve:* starve; 19-21: Though he has what he needs to help him (the lady) she doesn't help him. 25: To crave what is already his. 26, *lust:* pleasure, in this case, sexual desire. 30: The way hawks are trained. 33-35: He has good cause to say why he has reached this unhappy state. 34, *raught:* reached; 35, *hap:* misfortune.

56: This poem could well refer to the hazards of a love affair at Court. 1, *betime:* in good time; 11, *ween:* think; 18, *leave it in your lap:* tell you plainly; 19, *but a hap:* a rare occurrence.

57: 1, *intent:* intention, purpose; 2, *truth:* loyalty; 7, *tell can:* can estimate; 9, *assays:* trials; 11, *denays:* denials; 15, *mind:* intention; 19, *moved:* changed.

58: 5, *fain:* willingly, gladly; 9-10: 'Fire cannot be hidden in flax', proverb – i.e. Nothing can hide your love. 13-14: You cannot guide love in such a way as to prevent it expressing itself; 17, *For cause:* Because; 22: To be quit of the charge of love. 25, *fet:* fetch; 26, *wry:* conceal (B has 'wrap'); 27, *ne'er the nar:* never the nearer.

59: 2: To regard of little importance. 9-10: When you were well you could not stop yourself turning to love. 14, *Love's:* probably disyllabic.

60: I assume that in this poem the writer's despair, from which death offers the only escape, is caused by a woman, but the cause could be political. 5-7: Despair is so powerful that even that which most helps a person cannot withstand it. 8-9: Cannot withstand what is determined by the most extreme ill fortune. 10-14: To be worthy, but to be without her love (the law) or the liberty (of not loving) – in such a state what can remedy his thoughts of despair, of death? 12, *vaileth:* avails; 14, *vaileth naught:* accomplishes nothing; 19-21: Her disdain of him provokes him to suicide, which even the dread of death cannot prevent. 26, *kind:* nature; 27-28: To change his life from its present emptiness and despair to the 'place assigned' – hell. 31, *my restore:* my restoration – to the lady's favour.

61: 3, *fro:* from (somewhere else); 6, *receipt:* in receipt of; 8, *list:* chooses; 11, *mad:* E and D have 'made'.

62: 1, *th'eternal fire:* hell; 1-4: His love is like the thwarted desire of those in hell to see God. 6-7: Extreme circumstances similarly deny him 'the sight of her' he loves. 8, *puissant love:* mighty love.

63: 3, *wot:* know; 9, *careful knot:* the knot of love; 12, *spot:* deny or stain; 18, *swerve:* turn aside from his steadfastness; 24, *for no new:* for someone new.

64: *John Poyntz:* a friend and fellow courtier; 4, *thrall:* in thrall; 9, *strike the stroke:* to punish; 10-13: He has less esteem for the great than have the common people, who judge by outward appearance rather than by what is inwardly intended. 18: He cannot change his own honesty any more than black can be changed to another colour. 20-21: He cannot hide the truth to flatter those who don't deserve it and want to keep their vices. 33: He cannot hypocritically pretend that cunning is the same as prudence (counsel) and misuses words (paints them) for his own profit. 37, *state:* rule; 37-40: Cato, who also fought against Caesar, committed suicide after the battle of Thapsus (46 BC) rather than be captured by Caesar. 42: He was devoted to the common weal. 50-51: Allusion to tale of St Thopas and the courtly romance told by the Knight (Chaucer's *Canterbury Tales*). 52, *counsel:* prudence; 56, *points:* Is W punning on Poyntz? 59, *colours of device:* deceptions; 60, *mean:* the middle point; 61: A vice can be described as a virtue; 62-64: A virtue can be described as a vice, and so not recognized ('it may not rise') as a virtue, and he gives as an example, calling 'drunkenness good fellowship'. 67, *Favel:* A medieval personification of duplicity. 85: The novelty ('these news') of his country pursuits gives him neither a feeling of wellbeing nor of woe; 86: Except that, since his release from prison, he is in his father's custody ('a clog') in Kent. 88-89: But this confinement does not inhibit his liberty. 90: *delicates:* delicacies; 94-95: The good living of Flanders does not prevent him judging between black and white. 96: 'they think so highly of beasts that they think fit to make beasts of themselves' (Tillyard).

94

65: Addressed to Sir Francis Bryan, fellow courtier, poet, diplomat and intimate of Henry VIII. It imitates a satire by Horace, but is very much W's own, original work, although the manner and sometimes the language derives from Chaucer. 7, *eke:* also; 11-13: refers to Bryan's important work in matters domestic and foreign. He undertook a number of missions to France and to Rome. 16, *nappy:* foaming, heady; *nonce:* the occasion; 18, *groins:* digging with its snout; 19, *chaw:* chew; 21: Fx has 'As pearls to swine, so is good music to the ass', and draws attention to Chaucer's 'Artow like an asse to the harpe?'; 22: critical of cloistral life, 'sacks of dirt' = monks; 26, *list:* they please to do; 28, *wist:* know; 34 et. seq: sustained satire on the falseness, hypocrisy, deceit and insincere flattery of court life. 43-44: an obscure reference, meaning: don't lend unless you are going to profit by it. 45, *cant:* portion; 46, *leese:* lose; 47, *Kitson:* either Sir Thomas Kitson, a wealthy Sheriff of London or Anthony Kitson, a wealthy bookseller. 55: Hide from him the possibility of his death by treading on his spit. 57, *moe:* more; 57-58: without doing anything more to deserve it, becomes Executor. 60, *deburse:* disburse; 61, *rivelled:* wrinkled; 63, *ban:* curse, use angry language; 67-72: satirically, he is being advised to prostitute his niece, cousin, sister or daughter; 73, *ware:* be wary; 75, *Pandar:* Pandarus received no money for arranging Troilus's affair with Criseyde (Chaucer). 83-88: W's characteristic emphasis on the importance of truth and honesty. 90-91: W and Bryan were often in want of ready money.

66: Psalm 102 – Several lines compare closely with the text in Coverdale. 6, *intent:* attention; 10, *eke:* also; 18, *sprite:* spirit; 20, *solaine:* solitary; 21, *proper kind:* its own nature; 24, *waker:* wakeful; 33-34: God's wrath disdains his pride; 41-42: refers to original sin; 43-44: Zion here represents the people who live in accordance with God's law; 48: man's redemption by Christ; 49-50: in grief, or sorrow, to see Zion decay into dust; 57-58: To our descendants this written truth, of all comforts, will be the best consolation; 60: both the high and lowly shall praise the Lord; 63, *algate:* in every way; 64, *discuss:* set free; 65, *The sons of death:* those condemned to die; 66, *occasion gracious:* 'a reason resulting from God's grace' [Rebholz]; 68, *lauds:* praises; 72, *sembly:* assembly; 74, *dure:* endure; 78, *mids:* amidst; 79, *eterne:* eternal; 86, *erst:* first; 88, *pretend:* seek for, aspire to; 90, *in thy word are got:* are begotten in the word of God; 91, *stablished:* made stable; *all in fere:* all in friendship, companionship.

67: Psalm 130 – Several lines are closely related to the text in Coverdale. 3, *darkness' deep repair:* 'the deep haunt or resort of darkness' [M&T]; 4, *borrow:* deliverer, 'pledge, security' (Tillyard); 6, *overthrow:* ruin, or state of being cast down; 8, *intend:* pay heed; 10, *ne mayst:* may not;

14, *If just exaction demand recompense:* If justice requires the Lord to demand recompense for the offender's offence; 17, *large:* at large, completely; 22, *eterne:* eternal; 24, *pretence:* defence; 27, *thrust:* presumably 'thirst', but usually meaning pressure.